The Deat...

God's Will or Man's Folly?

The Death Penalty

God's Will or Man's Folly?

Robert Paul Martin

SIMPSON
PUBLISHING COMPANY

Simpson Publishing Company
Post Office Box 100
Avinger, Texas 75630

Printed in the United States of America

All scripture quotations are from
The American Standard Version of 1901

Library of Congress Cataloging-in-Publication Data

Martin, Robert Paul. 1948–
The death penalty : God's will or man's folly? / Robert Paul Martin.
    p. cm.
   Includes bibliographical references.
   ISBN 0–9622508–5–6
   1. Capital punishment—Religious aspects—Christianity.
2. Capital punishment—Biblical teaching.   I. Title.
HV8694.M33   1991   91-10761
364.6'6—dc20   CIP

Contents

Introduction

WHEN THE State of Florida executed serial murderer Theodore Bundy in 1989, for a brief time the news media focused the attention of the American people on the subject of capital punishment. As the date and hour of Mr. Bundy's execution approached, the public was subjected to a parade of legal experts, sociologists, politicians, and religious leaders, each asked to comment on the impending fate of Mr. Bundy in particular and the subject of capital punishment in general. The State of Florida, unconvinced and undeterred by its critics, carried out Mr. Bundy's sentence as scheduled.

The subject of capital punishment surfaced again on the national scene when a number of prominent politicians called for the death penalty for drug-related killings. This primarily was in response to public outrage at the murder of policemen and federal agents by drug dealers. Subsequently, legislation was passed in the Congress of the United States sanctioning the death penalty for drug-related killings.[1]

Perhaps at no time in recent history has more attention been given to the issue of capital punishment than at present. In legislature after legislature debate over capital punishment has been engaged. Public awareness and interest is high. Forces both for and against the death penalty have set them-

[1]See Pub. L. 100-690, Sect. 7001, 21 U.S.C. 848 (e).

1

selves in array to do battle over this emotionally charged issue. And to no one's surprise, each faction claims to have God on its side. During the Bundy affair, for example, religious leaders spoke both for and against capital punishment. Each side protests that God's will can be done only by codifying its perspectives into the law of the land.

Where should Christians stand on the issue of the death penalty? Among those who regard themselves as Christians, there is not a consensus as to the proper answer to this question. Some argue vigorously for the death penalty; others argue just as vigorously against it. Is there, however, a distinctly "Christian" position on capital punishment? I believe that there is, at least as far as general principles are concerned; and I believe that the foundation upon which the Christian view of capital punishment is to be built is the testimony of the Bible.

The approach usually taken in dealing with the question of the rightness or wrongness of capital punishment, even in many Christian circles, is to treat the subject philosophically and pragmatically. From this perspective, the attitudes and opinions of men are given priority over the teaching of the Bible. Such a treatment of the subject, however, produces nothing of definitive or absolute value to resolve the issue of the rightness or wrongness of capital punishment. At best, one ends up with a mass of conflicting statistics and a host of "definitive" studies by experts whose conclusions differ radically from one another.

My approach will be to view the question of capital punishment exegetically, that is, my sole concern is what the Bible has to say about the subject. The glory of the Protestant

Reformation was its summons to the people of God to form their views of religious and moral truth solely on the basis of the teaching of the Holy Scriptures. The Reformers and their followers insisted that every human opinion bow before the mind of God revealed in the Bible. Following the lead of the Reformation, my approach to the question of capital punishment will be to suspend the entire weight of the Christian position on the biblical data. With this issue, as with every other question of importance to Christians, the rule by which our opinions are to be judged is the teaching of the Bible. The teaching of the Holy Scriptures defines the "Christian" view of capital punishment.

Perhaps it will help the reader to know at the outset of this study that I am persuaded that the Bible supports the proposition that in the present epoch of redemptive history (i.e., under the New Covenant) God (1) mandates capital punishment for the crime of murder and (2) permits the civil government to punish other forms of aggravated evildoing in the same manner. In support of this proposition, I will (1) survey the biblical teaching on the subject of capital punishment and (2) consider objections ordinarily raised against the biblical position. I trust that as the reader considers the following pages, he will do so with a "Berean spirit" (Acts 17:11), that is, with an open mind, yet searching the Scriptures to see if my conclusions rest on a solid biblical foundation.

Part One

The Biblical Teaching Concerning the Death Penalty

Revelation Given to Noah

THE FIRST text in the Bible to address the subject of capital punishment is Genesis 9:5-6.

> And surely your blood, the blood of your lives, will I require; at the hand of every beast will I require it: and at the hand of man, even at the hand of every man's brother, will I require the life of man. Whoso sheddeth man's blood, by man shall his blood be shed: for in the image of God made he man.

This is perhaps the most important text in the Bible on the subject of God's will concerning the death penalty. Its pivotal significance derives from the fact that it records a divinely established mandate that God purposed would be in force as long as "the earth remains" (Genesis 8:22), "for perpetual generations" (Genesis 9:12). This command is a stipulation of the Noahic Covenant which still is binding on the present generation. Under the provisions of the Noahic Covenant, as long as the earth remains, God demands that murderers forfeit their lives as punishment for their crimes.

In order better to appreciate the strategic place that this text ought to have in our thinking, we must consider carefully the context in which it is found. The commandment recorded in Genesis 9:5-6 has an historical setting; and we must understand this setting in order to understand properly the commandment itself. What is the background historically against which this commandment was given by God? What conditions historically caused God to mandate the death penalty for murder for as long as "the earth remains"?

In order to understand Genesis 9:5-6 in its scriptural and historical context, we will consider the passage under four headings: (1) the place of the Book of Genesis in biblical ethics; (2) the history of two "seeds" recorded in the early chapters of Genesis; (3) divine revelation after the Flood concerning the perpetuation and preservation of human life; (4) God's revelation to Noah concerning the death penalty.

1. *The Place of the Book of Genesis in Biblical Ethics*

Before considering materials from the Book of Genesis itself, it is important to note the crucial role that the early chapters of Genesis play in a Bible-based system of ethics. In the opening chapters of Genesis, Moses records that at the beginning of history God revealed a number of fundamental principles concerning the morality which is to characterize the lives of those who were created to be the imagebearers of God. Preeminent among the divine revelations given to man at the time of his creation are principles concerning such things as marriage, work, and sabbath (Genesis 1-2). Later in human history, in association with the covenant which God made with Noah after the Flood (at the so-called "second Genesis" or second beginning of history), the Lord gave special commands concerning the sanctity and preservation of life. Among these commands is the divine ordinance which requires the taking of the life of the manslayer (Genesis 9:5-6). This, of course, is the ordinance which we are considering.

From the way that the Bible repeatedly refers to basic principles recorded in Genesis when addressing crucial moral issues, it is clear that these principles serve a foundational role in biblical ethics.[1] These principles are the foundation to which later divine revelations are added. These later revelations, however, do not set aside the basic revelation of God's will in Genesis; on the contrary, they confirm and expand the basic perspectives revealed by God at the dawn of history. We see this relation clearly, for example, when considering the so-called "creation ordinances." Later revelations only serve to confirm the will of God revealed at creation concerning marriage, work, and the sabbath.

This intimate relationship between principles revealed at the dawn of history and later revelations also applies to God's word concerning capital punishment in Genesis 9:5-6. This text is a record of foundational principles on the subject of the death penalty. Later revelations under the Mosaic Covenant and the New Covenant expand our understanding of God's will for the present epoch of history (i.e., the New Covenant era); however, these later revelations do not alter fundamentally the basic perspectives found in Genesis 9. On the contrary, the perspectives of Genesis 9:5-6 are confirmed by later revelations of God.

2. *The History of Two "Seeds"*

The early chapters of Genesis contain a brief history of two "seeds," i.e., two lines of the descendants of Adam and Eve, two lines separated as much by their moral character as by their genealogies. One of the dominant themes in these chapters is the continuing manifestation of sin in the human race after the fall of Adam and Eve. Genesis 4-6 describes the progressive moral degeneration of the race from the time of Adam to the time of the Great Flood in the days of Noah. One feature of this moral decline, the increasing manifes-

[1]See, for example, Mark 2:27; Matthew 19:4-6; 1 Corinthians 11:8-10; 1 Timothy 2:13.

tation of violent and murderous behavior, led not only to the Flood in the days of Noah but to the establishment of the death penalty as part of the Noahic Covenant. In Genesis 4-6, the Bible draws specific contrasts (1) between Cain and Abel—in the first generation after Adam, (2) between Lamech and Enoch—both in the seventh generation, and (3) between the generation destroyed in the Flood and Noah.

Contrast #1: Cain versus Abel. Genesis 4:1-8 contrasts Cain and Abel, the first generation after Adam and Eve.

> And the man knew Eve his wife; and she conceived, and bare Cain, and said, I have gotten a man with the help of Jehovah. And again she bare his brother Abel. And Abel was a keeper of sheep, but Cain was a tiller of the ground. And in process of time it came to pass, that Cain brought of the fruit of the ground an offering unto Jehovah. And Abel, he also brought of the firstlings of his flock and of the fat thereof. And Jehovah had respect unto Abel and to his offering: but unto Cain and to his offering he had not respect. And Cain was very wroth, and his countenance fell. And Jehovah said unto Cain, Why art thou wroth? and why is thy countenance fallen? If thou doest well, shall it not be lifted up? and if thou doest not well, sin coucheth at the door: and unto thee shall be its desire, but do thou rule over it. And Cain told Abel his brother. And it came to pass, when they were in the field, that Cain rose up against Abel his brother, and slew him.

This passage records the first murder committed in history. Abel's sacrifice had been accepted by God; Cain's had not (4:4-5). The Bible teaches that Abel was a righteous man who by faith offered acceptable worship to God; whereas Cain was an evil man whose offerings were the expression of faithless formalism.[1] In dealing with Cain, the Lord warned him that sin would seek to exercise dominion over him (4:6-7). Cain,

[1]See Hebrews 11:4; 1 John 3:12; Matthew 23:35.

however, did not rule over his sin. Full of jealousy and anger, Cain rose up and murdered his brother (4:8). In the first generation after the Fall, the Bible records a tragic case of flagrant and violent disregard for human life. With brazen indifference to the fact that his brother was a man made in the image of God, Cain brutally murdered Abel.

Contrast #2: Lamech versus Enoch. Following the account of the sin and judgment of Cain, Genesis records the history of Cain's descendants, the birth of his brother Seth, and the history of Seth's descendants. The contrast between these two lines of descent is as marked as was the contrast between Cain and Abel. With reference to the descendants of Seth, Genesis emphasizes the possession of special redemptive grace which manifested itself in "calling upon the name of the Lord" (4:26), "walking with God" (5:22,24; 6:9), and "righteousness" (6:9). By way of contrast, there apparently was no godly religion among the descendants of Cain.[1] This radical spiritual contrast comes into clearest focus in the seventh generation, i.e., in Lamech (in the line of Cain) and in Enoch (in the line of Seth).

Lamech manifested the violent and murderous spirit of his ancestor Cain. Note Lamech's arrogant song.

> And Lamech said unto his wives:
> > Adah and Zillah, hear my voice;
> > Ye wives of Lamech, hearken unto my speech:
> > For I have slain a man for wounding me,
> > And a young man for bruising me:
> > If Cain shall be avenged sevenfold,
> > Truly Lamech seventy and sevenfold.[2]

---

[1]Mention is made only of the agrarian, cultural, and industrial accomplishments of the sons of Lamech (4:20-22). These things may be manifestations of common grace but not of special redemptive grace.

[2]Genesis 4:23-24. "The history of the Cainites began with a murder-deed. It ends with a murder-song." Melancthon W. Jacobus, *Notes, Critical and Explanatory, on the Book of Genesis* (New York: Robert Carter & Brothers, 1872), 1:143.

Apparently Lamech believed that he had suffered an injury at the hands of a younger man. Lamech responded, however, with merciless and excessive retaliation, i.e., in response to a "wound" or "bruise" Lamech "slays" the young man. His triumphant song indicates that Lamech was devoid of any sense that he sinned in murdering the young man; on the contrary, the judgment of his conscience was so perverted that he was emboldened in his murderous course by the mercy which God extended to his ancestor Cain.[1] Lamech was a calloused, cold-blooded murderer.

In contrast to murderous Lamech, Enoch was a righteous man who "walked with God."

> And Enoch lived sixty and five years, and begat Methuselah: and Enoch *walked with God* after he begat Methuselah three hundred years, and begat sons and daughters: and all the days of Enoch were three hundred sixty and five years: and Enoch *walked with God:* and he was not; for God took him.[2]

What does the Bible mean when it says that Enoch "walked with God"? For the answer to this question, we must look elsewhere in the Scriptures. Hebrews 11:5 reads:

> *By faith* Enoch was translated that he should not see death; and he was not found, because God translated him: for he hath had witness borne to him that before his translation he had been well-pleasing unto God.

"Walking with God" (the imagery used to describe Enoch in Genesis 5) is the same as living "by faith" (the imagery used to describe Enoch in Hebrews 11). Enoch was a man of faith, that is, Enoch walked by faith, believing and obeying the revelation of God, trusting the God with whom he walked.

[1]See Genesis 4:15.
[2]Genesis 5:21-24.

We also learn from Jude 14-15 that Enoch was a prophet who stood for the truth of God and rebuked the ungodly of his day:

> And to these also Enoch, the seventh from Adam, prophesied, saying, Behold, the Lord came with ten thousands of his holy ones, to execute judgment upon all, and to convict all the ungodly of all their works of ungodliness which they have ungodly wrought, and of all the hard things which ungodly sinners have spoken against him.

Enoch was a man as distinguished by his faith and righteousness as Lamech was for his murderous wickedness. As Lamech was the embodiment of the irreligious and violent tradition handed down from his father Cain, so Enoch was the embodiment of the faith and righteousness of his father Seth.

Contrast #3: The generation destroyed in the Flood versus Noah. The biblical record of the descendants of Cain ends with Lamech and his sons. The record of the descendants of Seth continues down to the time of the Great Flood and comes to its focal point in the person of Noah. The character of Noah is described in three passages in the Bible.

> Noah found favor in the eyes of Jehovah. . . . Noah was a righteous man, and perfect in his generations: Noah walked with God. . . . And Jehovah said unto Noah, Come thou and all thy house into the ark; for thee have I seen righteous before me in this generation.[1]

> By faith Noah, being warned of God concerning things not seen as yet, moved with godly fear, prepared an ark to the saving of his house; through which he condemned the world, and became heir of the righteousness which is according to faith.[2]

---

[1]Genesis 6:8-9; 7:1.
[2]Hebrews 11:7.

> [God] preserved Noah with seven others, a preacher of right-
> eousness, when he brought a flood upon the world of the
> ungodly.[1]

Like his ancestor Enoch, Noah was "a righteous man" who
"walked with God" with a humble, submissive, and obedient
faith. The Bible records that Noah was "perfect in his generations." The perfection spoken of is not sinless perfection, of
course, but consistent moral integrity which manifests itself in
a walk characterized by a concern for scrupulous obedience
to all of God's commands. In his striving for universal and
scrupulous moral integrity before God, Noah was alone in his
generation. Noah also was a "preacher of righteousness." Like
Enoch before him, Noah took a public stand for the cause of
God and truth and reproved the ungodliness of his day.

In contrast to the righteous character of Noah, the Bible
displays the wicked character of his generation. Perhaps,
however, the most marked feature of this portion of the
Genesis record is the religious and ethical degeneration of the
descendants of Seth to the point that they are morally indistin-
guishable from the descendants of Cain. When Moses records
the history of Noah and his generation, no longer can he
contrast the wicked descendants of Cain with the righteous
descendants of Seth; rather, Moses contrasts righteous Noah
(the sole remaining godly Sethite) with the rest of humanity
(composed not only of wicked Cainites but also of equally
wicked Sethites). Genesis 6:1-13 reads:

> And it came to pass, when men began to multiply on the face
> of the ground, and daughters were born unto them, that the
> sons of God saw the daughters of men that they were fair; and
> they took them wives of all that they chose. And Jehovah said,

---

[1] 2 Peter 2:5.

My spirit shall not strive with man for ever, for that he also is flesh: yet shall his days be a hundred and twenty years. The Nephilim were in the earth in those days, and also after that, when the sons of God came in unto the daughters of men, and they bare children to them: the same were the mighty men that were of old, the men of renown.

And Jehovah saw that the wickedness of man was great in the earth, and that every imagination of the thoughts of his heart was only evil continually. And it repented Jehovah that he had made man on the earth, and it grieved him at his heart. And Jehovah said, I will destroy man whom I have created from the face of the ground; both man, and beast, and creeping things, and birds of the heavens; for it repenteth me that I have made them. But Noah found favor in the eyes of Jehovah.

These are the generations of Noah. Noah was a righteous man, and perfect in his generations: Noah walked with God. And Noah begat three sons, Shem, Ham, and Japheth. And the earth was corrupt before God, and the earth was filled with violence. And God saw the earth, and, behold, it was corrupt; for all flesh had corrupted their way upon the earth. And God said unto Noah, The end of all flesh is come before me; for the earth is filled with violence through them; and, behold, I will destroy them with the earth.

Moses describes the generation destroyed by the Flood in terms of universal wickedness. "And Jehovah saw that the wickedness of man was great in the earth, and that every imagination of the thoughts of his heart was only evil continually" (6:5); "the earth was corrupt before God" (6:11); "all flesh had corrupted their way upon the earth" (6:12). The Flood generation was intensely and habitually wicked, both outwardly and inwardly (i.e., in their actions and in their hearts).

One of the manifestations of the wickedness of the flood generation was that "the earth was filled with violence"

(6:11,13). The violent character of Cain and Lamech now has become characteristic of an entire generation. Yet even in the midst of a generation which was characteristically violent, some were more violent than others. Moses mentions the presence of the "Nephilim." This term is derived from the Hebrew word *naphal* (which means "to fall upon"), so that the "Nephilim" literally were "attackers" who "fell upon" other men violently. It is possible that Moses refers to the murderous highwaymen and muggers of Noah's generation.

How did God respond to the wickedness and violence of Noah's generation?

> And Jehovah saw that the wickedness of man was great in the earth, and that every imagination of the thoughts of his heart was only evil continually. And it repented Jehovah that he had made man on the earth, and it grieved him at his heart. And Jehovah said, I will destroy man whom I have created from the face of the ground; both man, and beast, and creeping things, and birds of the heavens; for it repenteth me that I have made them. . . . And the earth was corrupt before God, and the earth was filled with violence. And God saw the earth, and, behold, it was corrupt; for all flesh had corrupted their way upon the earth. And God said unto Noah, The end of all flesh is come before me; for the earth is filled with violence through them; and, behold, I will destroy them with the earth.[1]

The Lord was grieved that man had no heart for God. He especially was grieved that man was so violent and so disdainful of the sanctity of human life. Therefore, exercising his sovereign rights as Creator and Judge, God responded to mankind's morally degenerate state with retributive justice. The Bible records that Jehovah sent judgment on the earth in the form of a flood which was universal in scope.[2] God's

[1]Genesis 6:5-13.
[2]See Genesis 6:6-7, 12-13, 17; 7:4, 19-24; 8:21.

response to the ungodly character and the violent conduct of humanity was to destroy every living thing.

God did not, however, respond merely in judgment. He also extended mercy to righteous Noah and to his family. By this act of mercy Jehovah preserved the Sethite line through which he purposed to work redemption, i.e., the line through which the promised "seed of the woman" (Jesus Christ) would come.[1] After Noah left the ark, the patriarch's first act was to build an altar and worship God in response to the great mercy poured out upon him and upon his family. The Lord's response to Noah's sacrifice is recorded in Genesis 8:21-22.

> And Jehovah smelled the sweet savor; and Jehovah said in his heart, I will not again curse the ground any more for man's sake, although the imagination of man's heart is evil from his youth; neither will I again smite any more every thing living, as I have done. While the earth remaineth, seedtime and harvest, and cold and heat, and summer and winter, and day and night shall not cease.[2]

Jehovah resolved to perpetuate man's life "while the earth remains." He promised that he would not again visit the earth with a universal flood.[3] The regularity of the seasons and the regularity of the rising and setting of the sun are testimony to God's faithfulness to this resolution. God's promise is especially gracious in view of the fact that men continue to be wicked and violent and thus continue to deserve the kind of judgment which the Flood represented. We must not misjudge, however, the significance of God's forbearing to destroy

---

[1]See Genesis 3:15.

[2]For other examples of the translation "although" for the Hebrew *ki*, see Exodus 13:17; 34:9.

[3]The Lord did not state that he would never again visit the earth with a universal destruction. When God's work of salvation is finished he will destroy the present heavens and earth by fire. See 2 Peter 3.

the earth again. After the Flood, the Lord did not turn away from his concern to punish violent men. On the contrary, at the very moment in history that he promised he would not again destroy the earth by a flood (Genesis 9:11), he also commanded the death penalty for murder so that the earth would not again fill up with violence (Genesis 9:5-6).

The contrasts in the early chapters of Genesis between righteous men and violent men are remarkable, especially the contrast between righteous Noah and his violent generation. When we come in just a few pages to consider the significance of the institution of capital punishment at the time of the Noahic Covenant (Genesis 9:5-6), it will be helpful to re-member the historical context within which the ordinance was established, i.e., we must appreciate the fact that God established this ordinance in an historical context in which he had just expressed dramatically his righteous anger with violent men by executing an entire generation because of its violent character and conduct. Additionally, it will also be helpful to recognize that one of the reasons that God acted so decisively with violent men was to provide a peaceable and stable climate in which to work out his redemptive purposes.

3. *Divine Revelation after the Flood concerning the Perpetuation and Preservation of Human Life*

We come now to consider the more immediate context of the ordinance found in Genesis 9:5-6 mandating the capital punishment of murderers. After the Flood, God established the Noahic Covenant, which contained a series of commands concerning the perpetuation and preservation of human life. The command to execute murderers is one of those commands. Genesis 9:1-7 reads:

And God blessed Noah and his sons, and said unto them, Be fruitful, and multiply, and fill the earth. And the fear of you and the dread of you shall be upon every beast of the earth, and upon every bird of the heavens; with all wherewith the ground teemeth, and all the fishes of the sea, into your hand are they delivered. Every moving thing that liveth shall be food for you; as the green herb have I given you all. But flesh with the life thereof, which is the blood thereof, shall ye not eat. And surely your blood, the blood of your lives, will I require; at the hand of every beast will I require it: and at the hand of man, even at the hand of every man's brother, will I require the life of man. Whoso sheddeth man's blood, by man shall his blood be shed: for in the image of God made he man. And you, be ye fruitful, and multiply; bring forth abundantly in the earth, and multiply therein.

First, note that God reconfirms his command that man is to "be fruitful, and multiply, and fill the earth" (9:1). This, of course, coincides with the command given to Adam and Eve at the time of their creation (Genesis 1:28). God's original command to fill the earth with imagebearers of God (i.e., human beings) has not been voided by the fall of man into sin or by the judgment of the Flood. Indeed, in view of the universal judgment of the Flood, Noah now finds himself in a position similar to that of Adam, in that Noah has become *de facto* the father of the whole human race.

The commandment to fill the earth is part of the background against which God mandates the death penalty for murder. God's plan is to fill the earth with his imagebearers. The murderer acts contrary to God's purposes, in that he usurps God's sovereign rights and violently removes a divine imagebearer (i.e., his victim) from the earth.

Second, note also that at this time God gives man an enlarged provision for the sustaining of human life (9:2-4). At creation God gave both to man and to beast the right to use plants as their source of food (Genesis 1:29-30). Now, however, under the provisions of the Noahic Covenant, animals also are given to man for food. Man's dominion over the animals now includes God's permission to use them for food, with a restriction, however, against eating the blood of the animal (9:4). Under the provisions of the Noahic Covenant the life of an animal is not so highly regarded that man cannot kill it for food; nevertheless, its life is to be highly regarded. Man is not to eat that which is said to contain the animal's life, i.e., the blood. Man is not to eat animals in the way that animals eat their prey; on the contrary, man (even in the taking of the animal's life) is to regard that life with respect as the creation and property of God.

Does the prohibition against eating blood have any significance as far as helping us to understand the command against murdering men? I believe that it does.[1] The connection between the dietary provision and the death penalty ordinance is to be found in a very important principle—all life is God's property, whether that life is human or animal. In the case of the taking of animal life, this principle is clear from the fact that, although man has God's authorization to take the lives of animals in order to use them for food, yet man must do so in a way which reflects a recognition that he does so only by God's permission. The restriction against eating blood makes it clear that man has no inherent right to take animal life as he pleases; he has only a divinely delegated right

---

[1]Note the close juxtaposition of concerns in our text: "But [animal] flesh with the life thereof, which is the blood thereof, shall ye not eat. And surely your [i.e., human] blood, the blood of your lives, will I require . . . " (9:4-5).

which must be exercised within the restriction which God has set. In the case of the taking of human life, the capital sanction against murder makes it clear that man does not have an inherent right to take his neighbor's life. The man who murders his neighbor has taken God's property without God's permission and must make restitution for his theft with his own life.

4. *God's Revelation to Noah concerning the Death Penalty*

In the preceding pages we noted that divine revelation recorded in the early chapters of Genesis occupies a foundational place in biblical ethics. Furthermore, we saw that in these chapters Moses contrasted three generations of the righteous and the wicked—a contrast which underscored the violent, murderous conduct of the wicked. Moreover, we observed that God destroyed an entire generation because "the earth was filled with violence through them" (6:13). And we saw that after the Flood, in the Noahic Covenant, God established a series of ordinances concerning the perpetuation and preservation of human life. We must keep these observations in mind as we come now to consider God's command to honor and protect the life of man from the manslayer (Genesis 9:5-6). In order to appreciate the pivotal place which this ordinance should have in our thinking, we must recognize its context scripturally as well as the background historically against which it was established by God. Genesis 9:5-6 reads:

> And surely your blood, the blood of your lives, will I require; at the hand of every beast will I require it: and at the hand of man, even at the hand of every man's brother, will I require the life of man. Whoso sheddeth man's blood, by man shall his blood be shed: for in the image of God made he man.

From this passage the following observations are warranted:

a. *The death penalty is not man's invention.* God himself instituted capital punishment for the sin of murder. God himself "requires" (Hebrew *darash*, "demands") the manslayer's life, whether the offender is man or beast ("at the hand of every beast *will I require* it: and at the hand of man, even at the hand of every man's brother, *will I require* the life of man"). Capital punishment, therefore, is not man's invention; on the contrary, it is God's righteous ordinance. Contrary to popular opinion, capital punishment is not rooted in some kind of pre-civilized "primal revenge" on the part of man; rather, it springs from the sovereign institution of God himself at a specific point in human history (i.e., after the Great Flood in the days of Noah).

b. *Murder is an assault on God's image in the victim.* Geerhardus Vos rightly observed that "in [human] life slain it is the image of God, i.e., the divine majesty that is assaulted."[1] It is man's unique existence as the imagebearer of his Creator which makes murder such an aggravated crime in God's sight. And it is this truth concerning man's nature which God here sets before us as the reason for a capital punishment for this crime: "Whoso sheddeth man's blood, by man shall his blood be shed: *for [because] in the image of God made he man.*"

The presence of the image of God in man radically separates the moral importance of taking the life of a man from taking the life of an animal. In our day animal rights activists commonly speak of killing animals as "murder." Animals, however, do not bear the image of God; therefore, viewed biblically it is not murder to take the life of an animal. Man, on the other hand, is radically different from other creatures.

---

[1]Geerhardus Vos, *Biblical Theology* (Grand Rapids: William B. Eerdmans, 1948), p. 54.

Man was created to be the living and visible representation of the character of his Creator. Therefore, because of man's uniqueness as the imagebearer of God, human life has unique sanctity.

Before we can appreciate the seriousness of the crime of murder, we must appreciate something of what it means that man bears the image of God. When we assert that the Bible teaches that man is unique in that he bears the image of God, what are the features of this divine image? In this writer's understanding, the image of God in man includes at least the following features:

1. To be the image of God is to have a consciousness of personhood (i.e., an awareness of self or "I"), which exists in the context of (1) an awareness of others (including God) and (2) an awareness of the rest of God's creation.

2. To be the image of God is to have a mind or intellect, i.e., it is to have the ability to think, to reason logically, to observe, to understand, to know.

3. To be the image of God is to have the ability to do and to accomplish, including the ability to innovate (which probably is a representation of God's power to create).

4. To be the image of God is to have the ability to will, i.e., to plan and purpose, to desire and choose.

5. To be the image of God is to have the ability to feel, i.e., it is to have emotions such as anger, love, compassion, grief, etc. God is not emotionless. God feels! And man is a reflection of this aspect of God's character.

6. To be the image of God is to have the ability to appreciate beauty and order and to hate ugliness and disharmony. As imagebearers of God, men have aesthetic sensitivity.

7. To be the image of God is to have the ability to communicate verbally, in language capable of expressing one's

thoughts, purposes, observations, etc. across the wide range of human experience.

8. To be the image of God means that like God, man's consciousness of personhood, intellect, ability to will and to do, emotions and aesthetics, and communication exist in a framework of morality. Both man and God are moral beings. Man was created with a moral and ethical consciousness, i.e., a conscience which relates all of life to a standard of right and wrong (i.e., to a standard of righteousness, justice, holiness, goodness, and truth).

Man truly is a unique and remarkable creature, created to be the visible, living representation of the character of his Creator. Man thus has a unique and special place in God's created order. It is logical, therefore, to deduce that it is a crime of enormous proportions (especially in the sight of God) to violently take away the life of one's neighbor, with no more concern for his special status as an imagebearer of God than if he were an animal. The murderer treats with contempt God's special work of man's creation. Moreover, God's sovereign rights as Lord are usurped by the murderer, who sets himself in the place of God by deciding when and how to take the breath of life from an imagebearer of God. Of course, it is no marvel that, in an age marked by agnosticism and atheism, God's sovereign rights are little regarded. And in a climate where the biblical doctrine of the image of God in man is regarded with disdain, where man is regarded as a highly evolved animal (but no more than that), it is no mystery that men commit murder as though their victims were but beasts or that society treats their crime casually.

The image of God in man, of course, was greatly distorted by man's fall into sin. It is beyond our present purpose to elaborate on this point; however, it is important to recognize

that, notwithstanding the fact that sin has caused man to
become a twisted and distorted picture of his Creator, he yet
remains the imagebearer of God. When God speaks to Noah,
it has been many generations since the fall of Adam and Eve,
and God has had to destroy an entire generation because of
its twisted and perverted morality; yet God still describes man
as his imagebearer and he informs Noah that this fact still
renders human life particularly sacred.

Some argue that the dignity of the murderer as an imagebearer renders capital punishment unthinkable. They ask, "Is
not the murderer also an imagebearer of God? How then can
we take his life?" Former United States Supreme Court Justice
Abe Fortas, an opponent of the death penalty, affirmed, "I
believe that most Americans, even those who feel that it is
necessary, are repelled by capital punishment; the attitude is
deeply rooted in our moral reverence for life, the Judeo-
Christian belief that man is created in the image of God."[1]
Such a statement displays a very inadequate understanding of
the biblical teaching concerning the image of God in man.
The Bible does not regard the image of God in the murderer
as a legitimate reason to abandon the death penalty. When the
Lord told Noah that he required murderers to forfeit their
lives for their crimes, he knew full well that murderers also
were his imagebearers. Simply put, when one imagebearer
murders another imagebearer, God regards the dignity of the
victim as paramount. Indeed, the murderer forfeits his right to
claim his own dignity as an imagebearer as a defense against
being executed for his crime; he forfeits that right when he
ignores the image of God in his victim by taking his life. That

---

[1]Abe Fortas, "The Case Against Capital Punishment," in *The Death Penalty* (Volume
49, Number 2 of *The Reference Shelf*), ed. Irwin Isenberg (New York: The H. W. Wilson
Company, 1977), p. 107.

the murderer forfeits his ultimate right as an imagebearer of
God is borne out clearly by the fact that the murderer is to
suffer the same penalty that a beast would suffer.

> And surely your blood, the blood of your lives, will I require; *at
> the hand of every beast* will I require it: *and at the hand of man,*
> even at the hand of every man's brother, will I require the life
> of man. Whoso [whether man or beast] sheddeth man's
> blood, by man shall his blood be shed: for in the image of God
> made he man.

The image of God is no more protection against the death
penalty than if the murderer were a beast without the image
of God at all. The manslayer, whether man or beast, is to
suffer the same capital penalty.

c. *Man is to execute the death penalty as God's agent.* "Whoso
sheddeth man's blood, *by man* shall his blood be shed." As far
as we know from the Bible, this was the first time in history
that God gave to man authority to execute murderers. Prior to
this time no such authority had been given; thus, the
execution of Cain or Lamech, for example, would have been
a usurpation of divine authority. When God spoke to Noah,
however, he gave such authority to men, so that from this
point in human history onward men have both a right given
by God and a duty before God to execute murderers.

Who, however, is to discharge this duty? This is the business
of the civil authorities. Indeed, we see the civil government
exercising this role even from patriarchal times.[1] The Bible also
mentions, however, the "avenger of blood." The avenger of
blood was a near relative who sought to avenge the slaying of a
family member. The activity of avengers of blood predates the

[1]Moses, for example, fled from Pharaoh after killing an Egyptian taskmaster
(Exodus 2:11-15).

Mosaic Covenant, which recognized and allowed this practice, albeit under strict civil regulation.[1] After the period of the Mosaic Covenant, however, the Bible makes no mention of this activity. As we shall see later, the New Testament forbids private vengeance (Romans 12:19) and only recognizes the authority of the civil government to execute criminals (Romans 13:1-7).

Because of the juxtaposition of ideas in Genesis 9:6 ("Whoso sheddeth man's blood, by man shall his blood be shed: for in the image of God made he man"), it is probable that the image of God in man is not only the reason for the murderer's execution but also the reason for man being the executioner. Since man is God's imagebearer, he is to execute God's sentence, in God's place, as God's instrument. God has ordained that man is to reflect the moral image of God by standing in God's place and expressing God's moral outrage.

Opponents of capital punishment commonly object that the state acts as if it were God when it takes the life of murderers. In one sense this is an accurate observation, although the objection contains a gross misconception of the manner in which the state acts as God. The civil magistrate, when he sits in judgment, has been placed there by God to act as his agent. The magistrate, however, has not usurped God's authority; that authority has been given to him by God himself, so that when the state sentences and executes a murderer, it legitimately acts in God's place carrying out God's will.

d. *God demands the death penalty for murder.* Genesis 9:5-6 does not teach that God merely permits capital punishment for murder. Furthermore, God's word to Noah on this subject did not come in the form of a suggestion. On the contrary, God

---

[1] See Numbers 35, Deuteronomy 19, Joshua 20.

told Noah that he "requires" or "demands" that murderers be executed for their crimes:

> And surely your blood, the blood of your lives, *will I require*, at the hand of every beast *will I require* it: and at the hand of man, even at the hand of every man's brother, *will I require* the life of man. Whoso sheddeth man's blood, *by man shall his blood be shed*.

The manner in which God expressed his will to Noah on this occasion places this ordinance in the category of divine mandate. God mandates that murderers be executed for their crimes. Viewed biblically, capital punishment for the crime of murder is not optional; and a refusal to implement this mandate on the part of any society is flagrant disobedience of the clear and revealed will of God.

Genesis 9:5-6 clearly is a crucial text for establishing the Christian position on capital punishment. After God himself executed a violent and murderous generation in the Flood, he mandated that from then on murderers must forfeit their lives for their crimes. This commandment is part of a divine order established "for perpetual generations" (Genesis 9:12), for as long as "the earth remains" (Genesis 8:22); therefore, it is binding on the present generation of men made in the image of God. As long as the earth remains, God demands that murderers forfeit their lives as punishment for their crimes.

Even if no further revelation had been given by God, the case for the death penalty for murder could rest on Genesis 9 alone. God's revelation of his mind on the subject of the death penalty does not stop with Genesis 9, however; and it is to this further biblical testimony that we now turn.

Revelation Associated with The Old Covenant

IN ASSOCIATION with the establishment of the Mosaic (also called the Old) Covenant, God gave further revelation concerning the subject of capital punishment. For our present purpose, however, it is necessary to recognize that this additional revelation (mediated through Moses) is not of the same character as the revelation which God gave to Noah. The covenant which God made after the Flood was established "for perpetual generations" (i.e., as long as "the earth remains") and has never been altered, superseded, or abrogated; therefore, its provisions are still binding on mankind. The Mosaic Covenant, on the other hand, was established exclusively with the nation of Israel and has been superseded by the New Covenant established by Jesus Christ. The civil stipulations of the Mosaic Covenant are no longer binding because the Mosaic Covenant is no longer in force.[1]

While the civil ordinances of the Mosaic Covenant were binding only upon the nation of Israel and only during the epoch of redemptive history in which the Mosaic Covenant was in effect, nevertheless the revelation which God gave

---

[1]On the subject of the three great divisions of the Mosaic law (i.e., the moral law, the ceremonial law, the civil law) and their significance for the New Covenant people of God, see *The Westminster Confession of Faith* (Chapter 19) or *The Baptist Confession of Faith of 1689* (Chapter 19).

under the Mosaic Covenant is very helpful in aiding our attempt to formulate a biblical perspective on the death penalty for our day. Two principles are clear from the civil law of the Mosaic Covenant: (1) the capital sanction against murder which was established as part of the Noahic Covenant is repeated and qualified and (2) the death penalty is extended to crimes other than murder.

1. *The Death Penalty for Murder Repeated and Qualified*

Under the stipulations of the Mosaic Covenant, the capital sanction against murder which was established as part of the Noahic Covenant is repeated and qualified. Note the following passages from the Old Covenant in support of this affirmation. In the Book of Exodus we read:

> He that smiteth a man, so that he dieth, shall surely be put to death. And if a man lie not in wait, but God deliver him into his hand; then I will appoint thee a place whither he shall flee. And if a man come presumptuously upon his neighbor, to slay him with guile; thou shalt take him from mine altar, that he may die. . . . And if a man smite his servant, or his maid, with a rod, and he die under his hand; he shall surely be punished. Notwithstanding, if he continue a day or two, he shall not be punished: for he is his money.

> And if men strive together, and hurt a woman with child, so that her fruit depart, and yet no harm follow; he shall be surely fined, according as the woman's husband shall lay upon him; and he shall pay as the judges determine. But if any harm follow, then thou shalt give life for life, eye for eye, tooth for tooth, hand for hand, foot for foot, burning for burning, wound for wound, stripe for stripe. . . .

> And if an ox gore a man or a woman to death, the ox shall be surely stoned, and its flesh shall not be eaten; but the owner of the ox shall be quit. But if the ox was wont to gore in time

past, and it hath been testified to its owner, and he hath not kept it in, but it hath killed a man or a woman, the ox shall be stoned, and its owner also shall be put to death. If there be laid on him a ransom, then he shall give for the ransom of his life whatsoever is laid upon him. . . . If the thief be found breaking in, and be smitten so that he dieth, there shall be no blood-guiltiness for him.[1]

In the Book of Numbers we read:

And Jehovah spake unto Moses, saying, Speak unto the children of Israel, and say unto them, When ye pass over the Jordan into the land of Canaan, then ye shall appoint you cities to be cities of refuge for you, that the manslayer that killeth any person unwittingly may flee thither. And the cities shall be unto you for refuge from the avenger, that the manslayer die not, until he stand before the congregation for judgment. . . .

But if he smote him with an instrument of iron, so that he died, he is a murderer: the murderer shall surely be put to death. And if he smote him with a stone in the hand, whereby a man may die, and he died, he is a murderer: the murderer shall surely be put to death. Or if he smote him with a weapon of wood in the hand, whereby a man may die, and he died, he is a murderer: the murderer shall surely be put to death. The avenger of blood shall himself put the murderer to death: when he meeteth him, he shall put him to death. And if he thrust him of hatred, or hurled at him, lying in wait, so that he died, or in enmity smote him with his hand, so that he died; he that smote him shall surely be put to death; he is a murderer: the avenger of blood shall put the murderer to death, when he meeteth him.

But if he thrust him suddenly without enmity, or hurled upon him anything without lying in wait, or with any stone, whereby a man may die, seeing him not, and cast it upon him, so that he died, and he was not his enemy, neither sought his harm; then the congregation shall judge between the smiter and the

[1]Exodus 21:12-14, 20-25, 28-30; 22:2. See also Leviticus 24:17.

avenger of blood according to these ordinances; and the congregation shall deliver the manslayer out of the hand of the avenger of blood, and the congregation shall restore him to his city of refuge, whither he was fled: and he shall dwell therein until the death of the high priest, who was anointed with the holy oil. But if the manslayer shall at any time go beyond the border of his city of refuge, whither he fleeth, and the avenger of blood find him without the border of his city of refuge, and the avenger of blood slay the manslayer; he shall not be guilty of blood, because he should have remained in his city of refuge until the death of the high priest: but after the death of the high priest the manslayer shall return into the land of his possession.

And these things shall be for a statute and ordinance unto you throughout your generations in all your dwellings. Whoso killeth any person, the murderer shall be slain at the mouth of witnesses: but one witness shall not testify against any person that he die. Moreover ye shall take no ransom for the life of a murderer, that is guilty of death; but he shall surely be put to death. And ye shall take no ransom for him that is fled to his city of refuge, that he may come again to dwell in the land, until the death of the priest. So ye shall not pollute the land wherein ye are: for blood, it polluteth the land; and no expiation can be made for the land for the blood that is shed therein, but by the blood of him that shed it. And thou shalt not defile the land which ye inhabit, in the midst of which I dwell: for I, Jehovah, dwell in the midst of the children of Israel.[1]

In the Book of Deuteronomy we read:

Thou shalt prepare thee the way, and divide the borders of thy land, which Jehovah thy God causeth thee to inherit, into three parts, that every manslayer may flee thither. And this is the case of the manslayer, that shall flee thither and live: whoso killeth his neighbor unawares, and hated him not in time past; as when a man goeth into the forest with his neighbor to hew

---

[1]Numbers 35:9-12, 16-34.

wood, and his hand fetcheth a stroke with the axe to cut down the tree, and the head slippeth from the helve, and lighteth upon his neighbor, so that he dieth; he shall flee unto one of these cities and live: lest the avenger of blood pursue the manslayer, while his heart is hot, and overtake him, because the way is long, and smite him mortally; whereas he was not worthy of death, inasmuch as he hated him not in time past. . . .

But if any man hate his neighbor, and lie in wait for him, and rise up against him, and smite him mortally so that he dieth, and he flee into one of these cities; then the elders of his city shall send and fetch him thence, and deliver him into the hand of the avenger of blood, that he may die. Thine eye shall not pity him, but thou shalt put away the innocent blood from Israel, that it may go well with thee.[1]

Clearly, the ordinance established under the Noahic Covenant continues under the Mosaic Covenant. The Noahic ordinance is reconfirmed, however, with important qualifications. Perhaps the most important qualification is the distinction made between murder and accidental killing (and, of course, the establishment of the cities of refuge). We should not conclude, however, that this distinction went unregarded prior to the establishment of the Mosaic Covenant. Even where there was not specific legislation, the consciences of men surely would have drawn such a boundary. What is new under the Mosaic Covenant is that the people of Israel now have this distinction codified as part of the nation's civil statutes and that provision is made to protect the accidental killer from unreasonable and unprincipled revenge.

Although Old Covenant law distinguished between murder and accidental killing, as far as the penalty was concerned it did not appear to distinguish between degrees of homicide as

---

[1]Deuteronomy 19:3-6, 11-13. See also Joshua 20.

our modern judicial codes do.[1] When a killing was the result of clear intent to harm, the Mosaic Law treated the killer as a murderer. Intent to harm was presumed if (1) the killer lay in wait for his victim,[2] or (2) there was known enmity between the parties,[3] or (3) if a lethal weapon was used.[4] There is no evidence that killing in the heat of passion was treated differently than cold-blooded, premeditated murder.[5] Indeed, even one guilty of what we would call criminally negligent homicide was subject to the death penalty.[6] Only when death was truly accidental (when God is said to have delivered the victim into his killer's hand)[7] or when the homicide was clearly justifiable (e.g., as in the case of self defense)[8] was there no bloodguiltiness.

2. *The Death Penalty Instituted for Other Crimes*

Under the stipulations of the Mosaic Covenant, capital punishment also was extended to crimes other than murder. The

---

[1]See, for example, the current U.S. federal code stipulating the definitions of the various kinds of "murder" and "manslaughter" (18 U.S.C. Sections 1111 and 1112). According to the federal code, the key difference between murder and manslaughter is in the terms "with malice aforethought" (defining murder) and "without malice" (defining manslaughter).

[2]Exodus 21:13; Numbers 35:20,22; Deuteronomy 19:11.

[3]Numbers 35:20-21; Deuteronomy 19:11.

[4]Numbers 35:16-18.

[5]According to current federal law, a homicide committed "upon a sudden quarrel or heat of passion" is charged as "voluntary manslaughter" punishable by imprisonment "not more than ten years" (18 U.S.C. Section 1112). By way of comparison, we know that animals which kill humans do not premeditate their "crimes" but act out of "passion" (or instinct); yet according to Genesis 9:5-6 they must forfeit their lives for their actions. If acting "without malice aforethought" in a "sudden heat of passion" is not a legitimate defense for an irrational animal, how much less so is this an acceptable defense for rational men. An unwillingness to control one's passions (i.e., a lack of self-control in the face of temptation) is never regarded in the Scriptures as a mitigating circumstance in weighing the gravity of sin or in determining its punishment.

[6]Exodus 21:22-23, 28-30; perhaps Deuteronomy 22:8.

[7]Exodus 21:13.

[8]Exodus 22:2.

Law of Moses mandated the death penalty for the following crimes:

1. Sorcery (Exodus 22:18; Leviticus 20:27)

2. Idolatry (Exodus 22:20; Leviticus 20:2; Deuteronomy 17:2-7)

3. Blasphemy (Leviticus 24:16)

4. Usurpation of the Levites' duty respecting the tabernacle (Numbers 1:51)

5. Usurpation of the priestly office (Numbers 3:10)

6. Sabbath breaking (Exodus 31:14-15; 35:2)

7. Cursing or striking parents, or obstinate rebelliousness in children (Exodus 21:15,17; Leviticus 20:9; Deuteronomy 21:18-21)

8. Ignoring the judgments of the priestly and judicial authorities (Deuteronomy 17:12-13)

9. Lack of virginity in a bride (Deuteronomy 22:20-21)

10. Adultery (Leviticus 20:10; Deuteronomy 22:22)

11. Incest (Leviticus 20:11-12,14)

12. Homosexuality (Leviticus 20:13)

13. Bestiality (Exodus 22:19; Leviticus 20:15-16)

14. Rape of a betrothed woman (Deuteronomy 22:23-27)

15. Manstealing (Exodus 21:16; Deuteronomy 24:7)

These capital sanctions were expressions of God's will for the nation of Israel living under the Mosaic Covenant. It is fundamentally irrelevant, as many have objected, to affirm that the death penalty seems unduly severe as a punishment for some of these crimes (e.g., lack of virginity in a bride). Such objections give greater weight to human conceptions of justice than to God's revelation of what is right and just. All of these laws were appropriate expressions of God's righteous judgment against such evil-doing; otherwise God never would have mandated these penalties.

While these laws were expressions of God's will for the nation of Israel living under the Mosaic Covenant, we must recognize that they pertain only to that particular epoch of redemptive history. Thus it is improper to insist that, in the present period of redemptive history (i.e., under the New Covenant), the state must institute capital punishment for all the crimes which were so punishable under the Mosaic Covenant. Whether our nation continues as a secular state or whether (as many desire) it becomes a religious state regulated by the Bible, the United States is not Israel and the New Covenant is not the Old Covenant.

What is the significance of the Old Covenant materials for helping us to understand the subject of capital punishment in our day? Three lessons are particularly important. First, the Bible does distinguish between murder and accidental killing; therefore, our criminal codes should (as indeed they do) recognize that not all killing is murder punishable by death. Second, our criminal codes are too lenient on those who commit so-called "crimes of passion." The idea that the murderer who acts in the heat of passion is less responsible for his action because he did not act with cold-blooded premeditation is radically unbiblical. Third, and perhaps most important in the present historical context, the Old Covenant materials teach us that the capital punishment of aggravated crimes other than murder is not intrinsically contrary to the character of God. This observation is important because, as we shall see in the next section of our study, the New Covenant materials speak in general terms of the authority of the civil government to execute criminals.

Revelation Associated with
The New Covenant

T WO PASSAGES in the New Testament directly refer to
the subject of capital punishment: Acts 25 and Romans
13. These texts are very important because they confirm the
continuing validity for our own day of the ordinance established by God in the days of Noah.

1. *Acts 25*

The first New Testament text pertinent to our study of the
death penalty is Acts 25:11. The Apostle Paul had spent two
years in the Roman prison at Caesarea, charged with foment-
ing insurrection against the Roman authorities and with
profaning the Jewish temple at Jerusalem. Paul's case finally
was brought for review before the judgment-seat of the Roman
governor of Judaea, Porcius Festus. Acts 25:7-11 records:

> The Jews that had come down from Jerusalem stood round
> about him, bringing against him many and grievous charges
> which they could not prove; while Paul said in his defense,
> Neither against the law of the Jews, nor against the temple, nor
> against Caesar, have I sinned at all. But Festus, desiring to gain
> favor with the Jews, answered Paul and said, Wilt thou go up to
> Jerusalem, and there be judged of these things before me? But
> Paul said, I am standing before Caesar's judgment-seat, where
> I ought to be judged: to the Jews have I done no wrong, as thou

also very well knowest. *If then I am a wrong-doer, and have committed anything worthy of death, I refuse not to die;* but if none of those things is true whereof these accuse me, no man can give me up unto them. I appeal unto Caesar.

For our present purpose the lesson to be derived from this text is that Paul (who knew more about the Scriptures and more about the morality demanded by the New Covenant than any modern Bible interpreter) does not question the right of the Roman authorities to execute him if he is "a wrong-doer" who has done "anything worthy of death." In his own defense Paul raises no protest against the legality or morality of capital punishment; he merely objects that he is innocent of the charges levelled against him.

I believe that it is a valid inference from Paul's words to conclude that in his opinion, there were crimes for which the death penalty was appropriate. It is also important to observe that Paul speaks in general terms ("if then I am a wrong-doer, and have committed anything worthy of death"). He does not say, "if I am a murderer." The implication is that Paul recognized the right of the Roman authorities to execute criminals for crimes other than murder.[1]

2. *Romans 13*

The second New Testament text relevant to the subject of the death penalty is Romans 13:1-7.

Let every soul be in subjection to the higher powers: for there is no power but of God; and the powers that be are ordained of

---

[1]Compare also the attitude of the thief crucified with Jesus, as expressed in his rebuke of his fellow thief who was railing on Jesus: "Dost thou not even fear God, seeing thou art in the same condemnation? And we indeed justly; for we receive the due reward of our deeds: but this man hath done nothing amiss" (Luke 23:40-41). He regarded his execution for theft as "due reward." And he recognized the right of the Roman government to "justly" execute thieves.

God. Therefore he that resisteth the power, withstandeth the ordinance of God: and they that withstand shall receive to themselves judgment. For rulers are not a terror to the good work, but to the evil. And wouldest thou have no fear of the power? do that which is good, and thou shalt have praise from the same: for he is a minister of God to thee for good. But if thou do that which is evil, be afraid; for he beareth not the sword in vain: for he is a minister of God, an avenger for wrath to him that doeth evil. Wherefore ye must needs be in subjection, not only because of the wrath, but also for conscience' sake. For this cause ye pay tribute also; for they are ministers of God's service, attending continually upon this very thing. Render to all their dues: tribute to whom tribute is due; custom to whom custom; fear to whom fear; honor to whom honor.

In this text the Apostle Paul describes the posture which the Christian is to have toward the civil authorities. The Christian, as is true of every citizen, is obligated to submit to the governing powers and to conduct his life as a doer of good works. Moreover, the Christian is to live in this manner preeminently "for conscience' sake" (i.e., out of a sense of religious obligation to God).

Paul, however, not only describes the posture which the Christian ought to have toward the civil authorities; he also articulates several important principles concerning the identity and role of the civil government. It is this aspect of the text which is of present interest, i.e., as far as helping us to come to a Christian view of the death penalty. The following observations from the text seem warranted:

a. *The civil government is ordained by God and derives its power from God.* Translated literally, verse one reads "there is no authority except by [the direct agency of][1] God; and those

---

[1] The preposition *hupo* designates direct agency; as opposed to *dia*, which speaks of intermediate agency.

[authorities] which exist are ordained [or: determined] by [the direct agency of] God." Civil rulers do not exercise an inherent, self-originating authority; nor does their authority derive fundamentally from the consent of the governed. Rather, the governing authorities which exist are established by the direct agency of God himself and exercise authority delegated by God.

b. *The civil ruler is God's servant.* Paul says, "he is a minister (*diakonos*, servant) of God to thee for good." As God's servant, the civil ruler is solemnly obligated to do God's will. His own desires and the desires of the ruled are secondary to the will of his Master; and, where the revealed will of God differs from his or the people's opinions and desires, he must implement his Master's will in order to show himself a faithful servant of God. Although history is full of examples of wicked rulers who were unfaithful servants of God, this fact does not negate the truth that God established civil rule in order to serve his interests and concerns in the earth.

c. *The civil ruler is to punish evil-doers.* In his role as God's servant (i.e., serving God's interests in the sphere of rule delegated to him), the civil ruler is to encourage those who do good and to punish evil-doers:

> For rulers are not a terror to the good work, but to the evil. And wouldest thou have no fear of the power? do that which is good, and thou shalt have praise from the same: for he is a minister of God to thee for good. But if thou do that which is evil, be afraid; for he beareth not the sword in vain: for he is a minister of God, an avenger for wrath to him that doeth evil.

For our present purpose note especially that the civil magistrate is to be a "terror" (*phobos*, the occasion of fear) to those who do evil. Evil-doers are to be afraid because the civil ruler bears a sword for their punishment. The "sword" imagery, of course, includes the right to execute the death penalty. Commenting on this text, Professor John Murray observed:

> The sword which the magistrate carries . . . is not merely the sign of his authority but of his right to wield it in the infliction of that which a sword does. It would not be necessary to suppose that the wielding of the sword contemplates the infliction of the death penalty exclusively. . . . It can be wielded to execute punishment that falls short of death. But to exclude the right of the death penalty when the nature of the crime calls for such is totally contrary to that which the sword signifies and executes.[1]

d. *The civil ruler is God's avenger.* As God's servant wielding the sword against evil-doers, the civil ruler acts specifically as God's "avenger for wrath." The meaning of this phrase is that, as God's servant (or representative) implementing God's will, the civil magistrate manifests God's righteous anger (i.e., God's vengeance, God's wrath) against evil-doers. In the execution of evil-doers, therefore, the civil ruler does not express his own anger and vengeance or that of society; rather, he manifests the anger and vengeance of God.

e. *Punishment of evil is a deterrent to evil-doers.* Even as the execution of evil-doers was designed to express the anger and vengeance of God, so also it was designed to act as a deterrent: "But if thou do that which is evil, be afraid; for he beareth not the sword in vain." Potential evil-doers are to be afraid because the civil ruler bears a sword for their punishment. The clear indication of the text is that the promise of punishment is designed to deter men from doing evil. It follows, of course, that where the promise of punishment is an empty threat

---

[1] John Murray, *Romans* in *The New International Commentary on the New Testament* (Grand Rapids: William B. Eerdmans, 1965), 2:152-53.

(e.g., as with unenforced death penalty statutes), the deterrent value of the law is nullified.

f. *The sword is not just for murderers.* The general terminology used in this passage (i.e., Paul speaks of evil-doers generically, instead of murderers specifically) implies that the civil government's right to inflict capital punishment is not limited to the crime of murder. Other crimes may be judged by the state to be so aggravated or so heinous that capital punishment is ruled to be an appropriate response to them as well.

Summary: In broad strokes, what has our survey of the biblical materials revealed? First, at the time of the Noahic Covenant, God clearly mandated capital punishment for murder. This mandate is confirmed in the legislation of the Mosaic Code and continues under the New Covenant under which we now live. Second, the laws of the Old Covenant teach us that the Bible clearly distinguishes between murder and accidental killing. Third, the laws of the Old Covenant teach us that the capital punishment of crimes other than murder is not intrinsically contrary to the character of God. This perspective appears to carry over into the New Covenant era, with one difference, however. The Old Covenant mandated the death penalty for these crimes. The civil government in our day has no such mandate from God; however, it apparently has the God-given right to legislate the death penalty for heinous crimes other than murder. Therefore, for example, the legislatures of our land would appear to be operating within their divinely-delegated authority were they to legislate the death penalty for a crime such as drug dealing.

Part Two

*Objections Commonly Raised
Against the Death Penalty*

Biblical Objections

THE MAJOR objections which have been raised against the biblical teaching on the death penalty fall generally into three categories: (1) objections to the death penalty supposedly derived from the Bible itself; (2) moral objections commonly made by opponents of capital punishment; and (3) pragmatic or practical objections to the death penalty.

In the preceding pages we considered the primary biblical materials which establish the rightness of capital punishment. Opponents of the death penalty, however, commonly argue that there are other biblical texts which either negate or seriously call into question the legitimacy of the principles proposed above. In this chapter we will consider these objections supposedly derived from the Bible itself.

1. *What about the case of Cain?*

When Christians affirm that God wills that murderers suffer the death penalty as punishment for their crimes, frequently the question is raised, "But what about Cain?" The Bible records that Cain murdered his brother Abel; yet God did not require that Cain be executed for this crime. What are we to make of this? The record of God's dealings with Cain is found in Genesis 4:8-15.

And it came to pass, when they were in the field, that Cain rose up against Abel his brother, and slew him. And Jehovah said unto Cain, Where is Abel thy brother? And he said, I know not: am I my brother's keeper? And he said, What hast thou done? the voice of thy brother's blood crieth unto me from the ground. And now cursed art thou from the ground, which hath opened its mouth to receive thy brother's blood from thy hand; when thou tillest the ground, it shall not henceforth yield unto thee its strength; a fugitive and a wanderer shalt thou be in the earth. And Cain said unto Jehovah, My punishment is greater than I can bear. Behold, thou hast driven me out this day from the face of the ground; and from thy face shall I be hid; and I shall be a fugitive and a wanderer in the earth; and it will come to pass, that whosoever findeth me will slay me. And Jehovah said unto him, Therefore whosoever slayeth Cain, vengeance shall be taken on him sevenfold. And Jehovah appointed a sign for Cain, lest any finding him should smite him.

The first observation necessary to the proper evaluation of this objection is that in Cain's case God exercised his sovereign right to deal directly with the murderer. The Lord did not use any divinely established institution nor did he exercise his judgment on Cain through a divinely appointed intermediary, although he could have designated Adam as his "avenger for wrath" (to borrow the terminology of Romans 13) and commanded Adam to punish his son under the umbrella of the family institution. Instead, Jehovah dealt with Cain directly and personally.

The point is that the case of Cain is comparable only with those cases in history where God intervened directly and personally in passing judgment (for example, as we shall see later, the case of David). Ordinarily, God does not intervene directly and personally, but rather leaves the criminal to be judged by divinely appointed institutions or divinely authorized representatives.

The second observation necessary to the proper evaluation of this objection is that God did not institute capital punishment until many generations after Cain slew Abel, not until the time of the Noahic Covenant (Genesis 9). Before this time, God's permission to execute murderers had not been given; thus the execution of Cain by his fellow men would have been a usurpation of God's divine prerogative. This is why the Lord marked Cain as a warning against anyone taking vengeance upon him. Jehovah had not given to any man the right to act as his "avenger for wrath"[1]

In summary, Cain's murder of Abel occurred at a time in human history before God had granted authority to men to execute murderers. Subsequently, however, at the time of the Noahic Covenant, God established such authority; and this expression of God's will has been normative from that time until now. Simply put, the normative testimony of the Bible on the subject of the capital punishment of murderers is not the case of Cain but God's clear mandate in Genesis 9.

2. *What about the case of David?*

Objectors often refer to the life of King David of Israel to argue against the death penalty. According to 2 Samuel 11-12, David was guilty of two capital crimes, the murder of Uriah the Hittite and adultery with Uriah's wife Bath-sheba. The case of David is more complicated than that of Cain in that David's crimes were committed (1) after the establishment of the death

---

[1]Although God did not require Cain's life, Cain's punishment bore a very close relationship to his crime. See Genesis 4:10-16. Cain had stained the earth with his brother's blood. As punishment for this (over and above the curse already existing on man's efforts to till the earth, cf., Genesis 3:17-19), Cain is cursed to the point that the earth will not yield at all to his efforts to till it. Moreover, Cain is banished from the presence of the Lord, so that it is evident that his punishment is not merely material but spiritual as well.

penalty for murder in Noah's day and after its confirmation under the Mosaic Covenant and (2) after the establishment of the death penalty for adultery under the Mosaic Covenant. These ordinances were in effect at the time of David's crimes and yet David was not executed for either offense.

In studying this case, we need to recognize that David deserved to die for his crimes. Although God actually brought other judgments upon David, the Bible in no way gives the impression that he did not deserve to die; on the contrary, according to the Law of Moses, David was doubly worthy of death. Furthermore, the Bible does not record any mitigating or extenuating circumstances in David's case. Why then did he not suffer the penalty of the Law?

As with Cain, God exercised his sovereign right as the Supreme Lawgiver and Judge and intervened directly and personally, albeit through the use of his mouthpiece Nathan the prophet. God sovereignly set aside the death penalty in David's case and instituted other punishments instead.[1] Who would deny to God the right to do this? Mere human rulers (e.g., kings, presidents, governors) freely have exercised such pardoning power when it has suited their purposes. It is no great mystery then that the King of Kings and Lord of Lords also has exercised such a right when it has been in accord with his wise objectives. In any case, as with Cain, David's case is comparable only with similar cases of direct divine adjudication and cannot be used as a reason for overthrowing God's normative commandment in Genesis 9.

Some argue that David's case is unique in that he was an absolute monarch; thus there was no man with authority over

[1]See 2 Samuel 12:9-14.

him to execute him for his crimes. David's office, however, likely would not have protected him. Moreover, it is possible to deduce from Nathan's words that David expected to die: "Jehovah also hath put away thy sin; thou shalt not die" (2 Samuel 12:13). It is unlikely that the uniqueness of David's case derives from his office. It is more likely that the distinctiveness of David's case is to be traced to the divine promise made to him in 2 Samuel 7:11-16.

> Moreover Jehovah telleth thee that Jehovah will make thee a house. When thy days are fulfilled, and thou shalt sleep with thy fathers, I will set up thy seed after thee, that shall proceed out of thy bowels, and I will establish his kingdom. He shall build a house for my name, and I will establish the throne of his kingdom for ever. I will be his father, and he shall be my son: if he commit iniquity, I will chasten him with the rod of men, and with the stripes of the children of men; but my lovingkindness shall not depart from him, as I took it from Saul, whom I put away before thee. And thy house and thy kingdom shall be made sure for ever before thee: thy throne shall be established for ever.

This promise received its initial fulfillment in the birth and reign of Solomon, the son that Bath-sheba would later bear for David. Ultimately, of course, this promise was fulfilled in the person of Jesus Christ, the Son of David. Although David clearly was guilty of grievous sin, Jehovah was still sovereignly working his great purposes in history. God spared David's life in order to work out his sovereign redemptive purposes through David's posterity, most especially through Jesus Christ.

3. What about the woman taken in adultery?

Those who object to capital punishment on supposedly biblical grounds often point to the case of the adulterous woman brought to Jesus for judgment. Supposedly this case proves that the spirit of the New Testament is contrary to the implementation of the death penalty. This case is of special importance allegedly because on this occasion Jesus himself addressed the subject of capital punishment. John 8:2-11 records:

> And early in the morning he [i.e., Jesus] came again into the temple, and all the people came unto him; and he sat down, and taught them. And the scribes and the Pharisees bring a woman taken in adultery; and having set her in the midst, they say unto him, Teacher, this woman hath been taken in adultery, in the very act. Now in the law Moses commanded us to stone such: what then sayest thou of her? And this they said, trying him, that they might have whereof to accuse him. But Jesus stooped down, and with his finger wrote on the ground. But when they continued asking him, he lifted up himself, and said unto them, He that is without sin among you, let him first cast a stone at her. And again he stooped down, and with his finger wrote on the ground. And they, when they heard it, went out one by one, beginning from the eldest, even unto the last: and Jesus was left alone, and the woman, where she was, in the midst. And Jesus lifted up himself, and said unto her, Woman, where are they? did no man condemn thee? And she said, No man, Lord. And Jesus said, Neither do I condemn thee: go thy way; from henceforth sin no more.[1]

The main purpose of this text is to portray the scheming of the Lord's enemies and his wisdom in dealing with them. The scribes and the Pharisees did not come to Jesus as sincere inquirers desiring to receive instruction in the application of the penalties sanctioned by the Mosaic Law. Their only concern was to ensnare Jesus. They were looking for an occasion

[1]The genuineness of this text has been debated by textual critics and a strong case can be made against its being authentic. See, for example, Bruce M. Metzger, *A Textual Commentary on the Greek New Testament* (New York: United Bible Societies, 1971), pp. 219-22. For the sake of argument, we will regard the passage as authentic; however, if the text is not part of John's Gospel, its value to the objector is nil.

from Jesus' own lips to accuse him before the people. If they had been able to catch him expressing an opinion which could be construed as contrary to the Law of Moses, they would have been able to discredit him before the people of Israel. The purpose of the text, of course, is to highlight this scheme to discredit Jesus; its purpose is not to tell us about Jesus' view of capital punishment.

When Jesus finally responded to the question put to him, he said nothing contrary to the Law of Moses. Indeed, Jesus actually challenged the woman's accusers to stone her, i.e., he actually called on them to carry out the full penalty of the Law of Moses, on the condition that they could do so without hypocrisy. Jesus knew that they could not do this.

When her accusers left, Jesus dismissed the woman with a warning about continuing a life of sin. It is not correct, however, to deduce from this that Jesus abrogated the Mosaic sanction against adultery. Once all of her accusers had left, there was no case against her. Commenting on this text, George Hutcheson observed that Jesus "doth not make void the law of Moses, nor say that none ought to condemn her to death, but he declines to act the part of a civil magistrate in passing sentence upon her, and doth act the part of a minister of the gospel in absolving a humbled sinner."[1]

Even if Jesus (as part of his establishment of the New Covenant) set aside the capital penalty of the Mosaic Law for the crime of adultery, the Lord did not set aside the principle of the Noahic Covenant that murderers are to forfeit their lives for their crimes. The New Covenant replaces the Old (Mosaic) Covenant, but it does not abrogate the Noahic

---

[1]George Hutcheson, *Exposition of the Gospel according to John* (1657; reprint ed., Edinburgh: The Banner of Truth Trust, 1972), p. 160.

Covenant under which we still are living. John 8 has no bearing on the question of whether we are obligated by the Word of God to execute murderers.

4. *What about the Sixth Commandment?*

Often the Sixth Commandment "Thou shalt not kill" (Exodus 20:13) is quoted in opposition to capital punishment. For example, former U.S. Attorney General Ramsey Clark objects, "So long as government takes the life of its citizens, the mandate 'Thou shalt not kill' will never have the force of the absolute."[1] The logic of the argument from the Sixth Commandment is as follows: carrying out the death penalty requires killing the criminal; since the Sixth Commandment forbids killing, therefore, capital punishment is forbidden by God.

This objection to capital punishment is based on a profound misunderstanding of the Sixth Commandment. The Hebrew word *ratsach* (translated "kill" in the KJV, ASV, and RSV) here does not denote killing of every sort but rather that form of killing which we designate by the term "murder."[2] Therefore, a more accurate translation of the Sixth Commandment is "You shall not murder" (as in the NASB, NIV, and NKJV). This commandment forbids the unjust and deliberate taking of human life.[3] The commandment does not prohibit manslaying of every sort. For example, killing in self-

[1]Ramsey Clark, "The Death Penalty and Reverence for Life," in *The Death Penalty* (Volume 49, Number 2 of *The Reference Shelf*), ed. Irwin Isenberg (New York: The H. W. Wilson Company, 1977), p. 124.

[2]See the use of *ratsach*, for example, in Hosea 4:1-2; Isaiah 1:21; Jeremiah 7:9. In modern Hebrew, *ratsach* has come to designate "murder" exclusively.

[3]See George Bush, *Notes, Critical and Practical, on the Book of Exodus* (1852; reprint ed., Minneapolis: Klock and Klock Christian Publishers, 1981), p. 276 and Ezekiel Hopkins, *An Exposition of the Ten Commandments* (New York: The American Tract Society, n.d.), pp. 332-58.

defense is a just act. Moreover, accidental slaying is not murder because it is not the deliberate taking of human life.

With reference to our present topic, we need to recognize that capital punishment does not violate the Sixth Commandment. Capital punishment is not murder (i.e., a violation of the Sixth Commandment), just as the lawful seizure of property is not stealing (i.e., a violation of the Eighth Commandment). Though the death penalty involves the deliberate taking of the criminal's life, the civil magistrate is not on that account a murderer. On the contrary, the Bible regards him as God's "avenger for wrath" and God's "servant" who is performing a just act commanded by God himself in his Word.

It is clear even from the immediate context of the Sixth Commandment that capital punishment is not murder. In the very next chapter of the Book of Exodus, God commands that certain kinds of criminals are to be executed (see Exodus 21). Does the Bible prohibit murder in Exodus 20, while commanding murder in Exodus 21? No such confusion exists in the Word of God. The execution of criminals cannot be regarded as a violation of the Sixth Commandment, unless, of course, we are prepared to argue that the Bible is morally inconsistent with itself.

5. But doesn't vengeance belong to the Lord?

In opposition to capital punishment, some are fond of quoting Romans 12:19, "Vengeance belongeth unto me, I will recompense, saith the Lord."[1] The logic of this objection is as follows. By executing criminals, society takes vengeance on

---

[1]Similar words are found in Deuteronomy 32:35 and in Hebrews 10:30. Both of these texts, however, are part of sober warnings against the sin of apostasy. In both places God warns that he will take vengeance on those who repudiate the covenant which he has established. The issue of capital punishment is not in view in either text.

them for their crimes. If God reserves all vengeance for himself and if he assures us that he will recompense criminals for their crimes, then we must not execute criminals lest we usurp God's private prerogative. This logic is not supported, however, by the context of Romans 12:19. Romans 12:17-21 reads:

> Render to no man evil for evil. Take thought for things honorable in the sight of all men. If it be possible, as much as in you lieth, be at peace with all men. Avenge not yourselves, beloved, but give place unto the wrath of God: for it is written, Vengeance belongeth unto me; I will recompense, saith the Lord. But if thine enemy hunger, feed him; if he thirst, give him to drink: for in so doing thou shalt heap coals of fire upon his head. Be not overcome of evil, but overcome evil with good.

Romans 12:19 is part of a prohibition against private revenge. The Bible here does not forbid, however, the due exercise of the power of the sword by the civil authorities.

As with the preceding objection (i.e., with reference to the Sixth Commandment), a consideration of the following chapter will keep the objector from the embarrassment which his misuse of the text brings. If those who misuse Romans 12:19 would read Romans 13:4, they would discover that the Bible portrays the civil magistrate as "a servant of God, an avenger for wrath to him that doeth evil." Two principles are patent in this text. First, although the civil ruler is not God, he acts in God's place, with God's authority, doing God's will. Second, God instituted capital punishment as a means of exacting his own righteous retributive justice (i.e., his own vengeance) against evil-doers. Therefore, when the civil magistrate (as God's "avenger for wrath" and God's "servant") executes criminals, he does not exact the vengeance of society; he expresses the vengeance of God. No usurpation of God's prerogative is involved; on the contrary, the civil magistrate is the instrument by which God exercises his prerogative of vengeance.

6. *Doesn't capital punishment remove the criminal from the hope of conversion and salvation?*

Some object to the death penalty on the basis of what they believe is an overarching concern for the soul of the condemned criminal. Without question, of course, the souls of condemned criminals are important. And certainly we ought to appreciate the compassion which desires the ultimate salvation of those who have committed capital crimes. It is no mystery then that evangelistic compassion has led some to ask, "Doesn't capital punishment remove the criminal from the hope of conversion and salvation?" Many have concluded that the answer to this question is Yes. Along this line, for example, Professor Lewis Smedes has argued, "The death penalty is a foreclosure on the grace of God" for the murderer.[1] If Professor Smedes' observation is correct, then Christians who are seeking to be sensitive to all the teaching of the Bible have a very serious dilemma, i.e., how are we to square the biblical teaching concerning the death penalty with the biblical mandate to have compassion on the lost?

In response to this objection (and to the dilemma which it poses), several observations must be made. First, it is true that if a criminal is unconverted at the time of his execution, the death penalty removes him from the hope of conversion and salvation. According to the Bible there is no hope of conversion after death. And because of a penalty which terminates the criminal's life, the opportunity is forfeited to repent of sin and believe the gospel in the years which would have been his

[1]Lewis B. Smedes, "God's Will and the Death Penalty," *The Messenger* 45 (November 1973): p. 8.

had he not been executed for a capital offense.

Second, the sentence of death does not equate, however, with the absolute forfeiture of all opportunity to make peace with God through His Son Jesus Christ. Ordinarily there is a lengthy period of time between arrest and execution in capital cases. In the weeks and months and years usually required for the trial and the appeals which follow conviction, there is more than adequate time for a man to lay hold of Christ as his Savior. At the present time in America, the average length of the judicial process in capital cases is approximately eight years—more than enough time to reflect upon one's spiritual state and make peace with God.

Surely in such a case the motives to seek the Savior are as great as anyone can conceive. The condemned criminal faces a certain and near death for a heinous crime for which (along with the rest of his sins) he immediately must give account to the Holy and Righteous Judge of all creation. As far as the prospect of conversion and salvation is concerned, one wonders what good another ten or twenty or thirty years of life would do for a man who, in the midst of such circumstances, sees no need for a Savior from the wrath which immediately awaits him. What set of circumstances (humanly speaking) could possibly conspire to impress a man more concerning his need of salvation than those circumstances in which a guilty and condemned criminal finds himself? If anything, far from foreclosing on a man's opportunity to be saved, the circumstances in which a condemned criminal finds himself are as fortuitous as can be conceived of for a man to recognize his need of Christ.

Third, this objection assumes that society by its action can thwart the saving purposes of God. This objection is founded on the misconception that God desires the salvation of the condemned man, but ultimately does not control when or even if he will save him. The objector presupposes that the man's salvation ultimately is in his own hands and not in God's hands. If God is ready to save him but he is not ready to be saved, God's hands are tied. And by executing the criminal we take away from God further opportunity to convince him to cease resisting the divine overtures of salvation, thus, in the end, frustrating God's saving purposes. We tie the hands of poor, powerless God, who can only seek to persuade but who cannot actually save without man's permission. In a very real sense, from this perspective not only does the death penalty foreclose the condemned man's opportunity to be saved but it also forecloses God's opportunity to save him.

This perspective seriously impugns the sovereignty of God, who is as sovereign in his work of salvation as he is in his works of creation and providence. The Bible is abundantly clear that "salvation is of the Lord" (Jonah 2:9). Any number of texts could be marshalled to show that nothing man can do will frustrate the redemptive purposes of Almighty God; however, note the testimony of the Lord Jesus. Surely the testimony of the Lord Jesus Christ is to be received and believed. Jesus said:

> All that which the Father giveth me shall come unto me; and him that cometh to me I will in no wise cast out. For I am come down from heaven, not to do mine own will, but the will of him that sent me. And this is the will of him that sent me, that of all that which he hath given me I should lose nothing, but should raise it up at the last day. For this is the will of my Father, that every one that beholdeth the Son, and believeth on him, should

> have eternal life; and I will raise him up at the last day. . . . No
> man can come to me, except the Father that sent me draw him:
> and I will raise him up at the last day. It is written in the prophets,
> And they shall all be taught of God. Every one that hath heard
> from the Father, and hath learned, cometh unto me.[1]

Jesus spoke of a group of people given by the Father to the Son. "All" who comprise this group certainly "shall come" to Jesus and believe on him. Jesus said that it is the "will" of his Father that not one of those given to the Son should be lost. They will hear from the Father and will learn. And though unable to come to him in their own power, all of them without exception will be "drawn" by God's effectual (irresistible) grace, all of them will be taught of God, and all of them without fail will come to Jesus.

Where do we find room in Jesus' words for the theory that there are those whom God wills to save but yet cannot save because they are unwilling? Such a theory cannot be squared with the clear teaching of the Lord Jesus Christ. With reference to our present subject, either the condemned man has been given to the Son of God by his Father or he has not. If the Father has sovereignly given him to the Son, then he will listen to the Word and be taught of God, and he will come to Christ seeking the salvation of his soul. Though unable to come to Christ in his own power, he will be effectually "drawn" to Christ by God's sovereign and powerful grace; and no shortness of time remaining in his life can frustrate the divine will.

We see similar perspectives in Jesus' words recorded in John 10.

> The sheep hear his [the shepherd's] voice: and he calleth his
> own sheep by name, and leadeth them out. When he hath put

[1]John 6:37-40, 44-45.

forth all his own, he goeth before them, and the sheep follow him: for they know his voice. And a stranger will they not follow, but will flee from him: for they know not the voice of strangers. . . . I am the good shepherd; and I know mine own, and mine own know me, even as the Father knoweth me, and I know the Father; and I lay down my life for the sheep. And other sheep I have, which are not of this fold: them also I must bring, and they shall hear my voice. . . . My sheep hear my voice, and I know them, and they follow me: and I give unto them eternal life; and they shall never perish, and no one shall snatch them out of my hand. My Father, who hath given them unto me, is greater than all; and no one is able to snatch them out of the Father's hand.[1]

The Good Shepherd says, "I know mine own, and mine own know me . . . and I lay down my life for the sheep." Because Christ lays down his life for his sheep, therefore, "they shall never perish" in their sins. Moreover, the Good Shepherd "must bring" all his sheep into the fold; and by his powerful (effectual, irresistible) grace, he will gather all the sheep for whom he lays down his life. The result of this sovereign and powerful operation of grace is that every sheep without exception hears and believes and follows the Good Shepherd. Not one of Christ's sheep will follow the voice of a stranger. Not one of all that the Father has given to Christ will be missing at the last day. The Father has given them to Christ and he will give to all of them eternal life and not one of them will perish.

Again we must ask, where does the theory that capital punishment forecloses God's grace fit into Jesus' words? If the condemned criminal is a sheep given to the Good Shepherd, can he be snatched out of the hand of the Father and the

[1]John 10:3-5, 14-16, 27-29.

Son? If he is Christ's sheep (a gift to the Son from his Father), though the time is ever so short, then the Good Shepherd knows him, he will hear the Good Shepherd's voice and follow him, he will never perish, and no one (not even the executioner) will be able to snatch him out of the hand of the Father and the Son.

Christ will receive the fruit of his suffering and God's purposes in salvation will be completely fulfilled. Jehovah's Servant will "see of the travail of his soul and be satisfied" (Isaiah 53:11). God has not left the results of redemption to be decided by men. On the contrary, God sovereignly exerts his own power to assure that not one of those given to his Son will be lost but that all his sheep will come to him. The Jehovah of the Bible is not a frustrated God who at best has only partially succeeded in his saving work but who by and large has failed because of the unwillingness of men to be saved. Man cannot defeat the will and power of Almighty God.

> For as the rain cometh down and the snow from heaven, and returneth not thither, but watereth the earth, and maketh it bring forth and bud, and giveth seed to the sower and bread to the eater; so shall my word be that goeth forth out of my mouth: it shall not return unto me void, but it shall accomplish that which I please, and it shall prosper in the thing whereto I send it.[1]

> [The Most High] doeth according to his will in the army of heaven, and among the inhabitants of the earth [i.e., there is no difference in his sovereignty over angels and men]; and none can stay his hand [i.e., none can stop his powerful working], or say unto him, What doest thou [i.e., none can call his sovereign will into question]?[2]

---

[1]Isaiah 55:10-11.
[2]Daniel 4:35.

In reality, the objection to capital punishment which we have been considering destroys the very gospel for which it claims priority. The unspoken premise lying behind this objection (i.e., that an elect sinner can have his day of grace foreclosed before his divine election results in the application of redeeming grace) contains within it nothing less than the overthrow of the biblical gospel. If God is unable to deliver his elect, there is no "good news" in Jesus Christ.

This does not mean that Christians should neglect witnessing to condemned men. We ought to bring every possible motive and appeal to bear upon them, pleading with them to flee from the wrath to come. The one thing, however, that we cannot do and still remain faithful to the Word of God is set aside the clear mandate of the Bible concerning capital punishment. The Lord knows those that are his and he will without fail bring all of them into the fold. Christ does not require that we disobey or abrogate his Word in order to help him gather his sheep.

Moral Objections

IN THE PRECEDING chapter we considered objections to capital punishment supposedly arising from the Bible itself. In this chapter we will consider objections which are rooted not in the moral perspectives of the Bible but in moral perspectives which are widely held in modern society.

1. *The death penalty has no place in a civilized society.*

Opponents of capital punishment commonly object that the death penalty, especially when used as an instrument of vengeance, is uncivilized. Justice Fortas, for example, argued:

> It is wrong for the state to kill offenders. . . . In exchange for the pointless exercise of killing a few people each year, we expose our society to brutalization; we lower the essential value that is the basis of our civilization: a pervasive, unqualified respect for life. . . . Why, when we have bravely and nobly progressed so far in the recent past to create a decent, humane society, must we perpetuate the senseless barbarism of official murder?[1]

In a similar vein, former U.S. Attorney General Ramsey Clark remarked, "Surely the abolition of the death penalty is a major milestone in the long road up from barbarism."[2] Professor Charles Black of Yale protested, "I am revolted by

[1]Fortas, pp. 116-17.
[2]Clark, p. 123.

63

the idea of retribution through officially imposed death."[1] In like manner, columnist Clair Rees affirmed, "Retribution has no place in a civilized society."[2] What shall we say in response to such objections?

Certainly, God did not institute capital punishment as an outlet for man's spirit of retribution or vengeance. As we saw above (in our consideration of Romans 12:19), vengeance is forbidden to man. God, however, has not forfeited his right to exact divine vengeance on evildoers. Indeed, as Romans 13:4 clearly teaches, God instituted capital punishment as one means for exacting his righteous retributive justice (his vengeance, his wrath) on evildoers. Therefore, if the objection is that private or even corporate (societal) revenge has no place in a civilized society, then we must agree. If, however, the objection is that there is no place in civilized society for God's righteous retributive justice, then we must protest vigorously. The concept of punishment-as-just-desert is basic to the idea of civilization. How much more so is this true when the punishment in view is divinely mandated.

Can a society be regarded as "civilized" when it denies to God his own prerogatives? A society which disobeys God is not "civilized" but "pagan." If God's retributive justice has no place in "civilized" society, then most likely there is no place for God himself in such a society either. Sadly, of course, this is the present state of many of the nations of the earth. They have no place for God or for his will. Whatever may have been true of nations like England and the United States in centuries past,

---

[1] Charles L. Black, Jr. *Capital Punishment: the Inevitability of Caprice and Mistake* (New York: W. W. Norton & Company, 1974), p. 23.

[2] Nelson-Rees Survey: Stop Capital Punishment? *Lakeland Today*, 13 January 1988, p. 19. A dialogue between Clair Rees (pro) and Lee Nelson (con).

apparently many of the nations of the earth have become too "civilized" to obey God.

2. *Capital punishment is not administered uniformly and impartially.*

It is frequently objected that capital punishment ought to be abolished because it hasn't been administered uniformly and impartially. In response to this objection, we must acknowledge that there has been discrimination in the application of the death penalty. It is undeniable that in some jurisdictions historically there has been a pattern manifested in which poor defendants and men and blacks have received different treatment by the courts than rich defendants and women and whites. And this kind of discrimination ought to be condemned. In defending the death penalty, in no way are we defending the perversion of justice caused by discrimination in its application.

When God instituted the death penalty, however, he was not unaware that it would be imperfectly administered. In fact, God established the death penalty knowing full well that its application would be tainted by sin. Man's maladministration of the death penalty has not caught God by surprise. He is the God who knows the end from the beginning; and yet, notwithstanding his knowledge that men would administer his ordinance imperfectly, he established the death penalty. If God, knowing the facts, has not abolished this ordinance, are we then at liberty to do what God has not done? Are we wiser than God? Are we more righteous and just than he?

Furthermore, is it not clear to any thinking person that if the only divine ordinances to be embraced are those which cannot be touched by human sinfulness, then every divine institution must be abolished? On this premise we would need to abolish the home, the state, and the church, because historically those who have ruled in these spheres of divinely delegated authority often have exercised their mandates with great selfishness and prejudice. Moreover, if this logic is followed, we would have to eliminate all criminal penalties, not just the death penalty.

What shall we do in the face of prejudice and injustice in applying the death penalty? Certainly, legal reforms and safeguards are part of the answer. No set of reforms, however, can eliminate every vestige of discrimination from the judicial process. As long as men are administering justice, there will be imperfections and prejudice. The proper response, however, clearly is not disobedience to God.

3. *There is the possibility of the irreversible error of executing innocent people.*

Another common moral objection to the death penalty derives from the possibility that innocent people will be executed. Given the fact that the death penalty is irreversible, it is argued that even the possibility of committing such a grave injustice against innocent defendants makes the death penalty unthinkable. How shall we respond to this very important objection?

First, while we admit that it is possible that a person may be executed for a crime that he did not commit, given the careful judicial process in capital cases, including an elaborate appeals system (in the USA averaging eight years in length), such cases are extremely rare. Of course, death penalty opponents give the impression that innocent people are being sentenced to death on a regular basis. This is simply not the case. Professor James Q. Wilson of Harvard University remarked:

The chief cost of the death penalty is thought to be the possibility of erroneously executing an innocent man. But even as ardent an abolitionist as [Hugo Adam] Bedau does not claim that we have paid that cost very often. In 1962, he compiled a list of 74 cases since 1893 in which a wrongful conviction for murder is alleged to have occurred in this country. . . . In only eight of the 74 cases was the death sentence carried out (there have been more than 7,000 executions in this century); in the majority of cases no death sentence was even imposed. Writing in 1971, Bedau stated that no further instances of erroneous execution had occurred since his earlier review and concluded that it is "false sentimentality to argue that the death penalty should be abolished because of the abstract possibility that an innocent person might be executed, when the record fails to disclose that such cases occur."[1]

Second, when he instituted capital punishment, God was not unaware of the possibility of innocent men suffering unjustly. The Bible does not record, however, that God had afterthoughts about this ordinance, to the effect that he should have thought of this possibility before establishing the death penalty. As with the preceding objection, we must recognize that Jehovah is the God who knows the end from the beginning; and yet, notwithstanding his knowledge that on occasion the innocent would suffer unjustly, he established the death penalty. Again we must ask, if God, knowing the facts, has not abolished this ordinance, are we then at liberty to do what God has not done? Are we wiser than God? Are we more righteous and just than he?

Third, we must recognize that even in the execution of an innocent person, as lamentable as that would be, God still is

[1]James Q. Wilson, "The Continuing Controversy" in *The Death Penalty* (Volume 49, Number 2 of *The Reference Shelf*), ed. Irwin Isenberg (New York: The H.W. Wilson Company, 1977), pp. 144-45.

working out his sovereign purposes for that person. There have been thousands of martyrs whose lives have been unjustly taken away; and yet who would deny that God was working out his sovereign will for them through their martyrdom? Jesus was the innocent victim par excellence of Roman capital punishment, yet God was working out his sovereign purposes even through the culpable injustice and the supposedly "irreversible error" of the Romans.[1] Likewise, multitudes have perished as innocent victims at the hands of wicked men; and yet, although God was not the author of the sin which took their lives (for which their murderers must give account to God), God still was carrying out his sovereign decree. My point is that even in the case of the death of an innocent man at the hand of the executioner, God does not forfeit his place as the One who "worketh all things after the counsel of his will" (Ephesians 1:11).

Fourth, if we follow out the logic of this objection, no crime could be punished, lest an innocent man pay the penalty for a crime that he did not commit. Could we sentence convicted robbers to prison, knowing the possibility exists that someone might be unjustly convicted? Could we sentence rapists, extortioners, arsonists, etc., knowing that occasionally the innocent might be imprisoned? One can easily see that if this kind of objection is to regulate our judicial thinking, then the entire penal system must be abolished, not just the death penalty.

---

[1]Peter charged the Jews, "him [Christ], being delivered up by the determinate counsel and foreknowledge of God, ye by the hand of lawless men did crucify and slay" (Acts 2:23). Reflecting on the crucifixion of Jesus, the testimony of the apostolic church was that "of a truth in this city against thy [i.e., God's] holy Servant Jesus, whom thou didst anoint, both Herod and Pontius Pilate, with the Gentiles and the peoples of Israel, were gathered together, to do whatsoever thy hand and thy counsel foreordained to come to pass" (Acts 4:27-28).

4. There is not enough "due process of law" in our judicial system to make it an acceptable instrument for the "deprivation of life."

Perhaps the most eloquent framer of this objection is Professor Charles Black of Yale. Black argued:

> In one way or another, the official choices—by prosecutors, judges, juries, and governors—that divide those who are to die from those who are to live are on the whole not made, and cannot be made, under standards that are consistently meaningful and clear, but that they are often made, and in the foreseeable future will continue often to be made, under no standards at all or under pseudo-standards without discoverable meaning. My further (and closely connected) assertion is that mistake in these choices is fated to occur.[1]

Fundamentally, this objection is based on the morality expressed in the Fourteenth Amendment to the Constitution of the United States, which reads in part: "No State shall . . . deprive any person of life, liberty, or property without due process of law."

In order to object to the death penalty in this way, of course, one must make the case that the death penalty (i.e., deprivation of life) is in a class so apart from other punishments (i.e., deprivation of property or liberty) that the degree of "due process" acceptable for lesser crimes is unacceptable in capital cases. Professor Black seeks to make such a case, arguing that the death penalty is, in every sense of the word, irrevocable. This being the case, "we ought not to accept, with respect to the death penalty, the arbitrariness and fallibility in decision which we must accept, and will no doubt go on accepting, with regard to other punishments."[2]

---

[1] Black, p. 21.
[2] Ibid., p. 30.

How shall we respond to this objection? First, we must acknowledge the unique irrevocability of the death penalty. Yet we must also recognize that it is this feature which renders it such a suitable punishment for murder. As Professor Ernest van den Haag of New York University observed, justice demands that "the penalty must be appropriate to the serious-ness of the crime."[1] No other punishment meets the divinely established requirement of just retribution: "Whoso sheddeth man's blood, by man shall his blood be shed" (Genesis 9:6).

Second, is it accurate to affirm, as Black does, that "though the justice of God may indeed ordain that some should die, the justice of man is altogether and always insufficient for saying who these may be"[2]? Black is likely correct in observing that in the American system of criminal justice there is too much "standardless discretion" on the part of prosecutors, judges, juries, and governors (especially with reference to such things as plea bargaining and insanity defenses); but can it be true that "it cannot be reformed enough" to give accept-able due process in capital cases?[3] One's answer to this question depends on one's standard for measuring "due process." If by "due process of law" Professor Black means "perfect process of law" (and this seems to be the clear impli-cation of the language which he has chosen), he is begging the question. As long as men are administering justice, some level of imperfection in "due process of law" is unavoidable. God, of course, knew this when he demanded, "Whoso sheddeth man's blood, by man shall his blood be shed"

---

[1] Interview with Ernest van den Haag, in *The Death Penalty* (Volume 49, Number 2 of *The Reference Shelf*), ed. Irwin Isenberg (New York: The H.W. Wilson Company, 1977), p. 135.
[2] Black, p. 96.
[3] Ibid., p. 92.

(Genesis 9:6); yet he did not refrain from mandating the death penalty for murder. Every effort ought to be made to make our judicial system fair in its judgments; yet, in the final analysis, if we cannot achieve perfection in its implementation, we must not abandon the ordinance of God.

Pragmatic Objections

IN THE TWO preceding chapters we considered common "biblical" and "moral" objections to the death penalty. In this chapter we come to consider what I am calling "pragmatic" or "practical" objections. These objections are not derived from the Bible or from the moral scruples of the objector; rather, the objector here opposes the death penalty because "it doesn't work" or, given other factors, "it isn't worth doing."

1. *The data proves that the death penalty isn't a deterrent; and if it doesn't deter criminals, it isn't worth doing.*

Opponents of the death penalty regularly refer to statistical evidence which (they assert) proves that capital punishment does not deter criminals from committing crimes. They use these statistics to argue that since the death penalty doesn't deter criminals (especially murderers), then it isn't worth having as part of the judicial arsenal against crime. Typical is the comment of Justice Fortas:

> Practically all scholars and experts agree that capital punishment cannot be justified as a significantly useful instrument of law enforcement or of penology. There is no evidence that it reduces the serious crimes to which it is addressed.[1]

[1]Fortas, p. 110.

The statistical studies of Thorsten Sellin especially were important as far as shaping opinion concerning the deterrent value of the death penalty.[1] One writer observed concerning Sellin's work:

> Sellin's findings . . . came to be taken as dogma. People said "capital punishment doesn't deter murderers" with the same self-assurance that they might say "the earth revolves around the sun."[2]

What shall we say to this objection, supposedly backed by empirical data? At the outset, we need to recognize that there are others whose statistical studies have led them to conclude that the death penalty does deter. Former Indiana Attorney General Theodore L. Sendak, for example, affirmed, "Only misguided emotionalism, and not facts, dispute the truth that the death penalty is a deterrent to capital crime."[3] So heated has been the statistical warfare, with opponents and proponents of the death penalty hurling lightning bolt after lightning bolt of statistics at one another, that it has been called "the battle of the wizards."[4]

The simple truth is that, as with most statistical studies of this sort, the data is so ambiguous that one can reach radically differing conclusions depending on the methodology which one employs. Furthermore, the data concerning the deterrent effect of capital punishment for the most recent decades is

---

[1]Thorsten Sellin, *The Death Penalty* (Philadelphia: The American Law Institute, 1959).

[2]Frank G. Carrington, *Neither Cruel Nor Unusual* (New Rochelle, NY: Arlington House Publishers, 1978), p. 88.

[3]Theodore L. Sendak, "How about the Victim?" in *The Death Penalty* (Volume 49, Number 2 of *The Reference Shelf*), ed. Irwin Isenberg (New York: The H. W. Wilson Company, 1977), p. 132.

[4]Carrington, p. 88.

misleading because of unenforced death penalty laws. As
Justice Fortas observed:

> In fact, the statistical possibility of execution for a capital offense
> is extremely slight. . . . [Even] in the peak year of 1933 [i.e., the
> year of the highest recorded number of executions], there were
> only 199 executions in the United States, while the average
> number of homicides in all of the states authorizing capital
> punishment for 1932-33 was 11,579.
>
> A potential murderer who rationally weighed the possibility of
> punishment by death . . . would figure that he has considerably
> better than a 98 per-cent chance of avoiding execution in the
> average capital punishment state. In the years from 1960 to
> 1967 [i.e., the years leading up to the 1967 moratorium on
> executions pending Supreme Court resolution of pending
> capital cases], his chances of escaping execution were better
> than 99.5 per-cent. The professional or calculating murderer is
> not apt to be deterred by such odds.[1]

It is begging the question to argue that the death penalty
doesn't deter murderers, when the data being used to form
this conclusion is the number of murders committed in a
period when the existing death penalty laws were not enforced. It should be evident that a law without teeth is not a
deterrent.

The statistical issue, however, has a more serious problem
than the ambiguity of the data. Frank Carrington stated the
real statistical issue when he wrote:

> No airtight mathematical proof for or against the deterrent
> value of capital punishment is available to us now . . . .
>
> The basic reason for the lack of certainty in the statistical battle
> is obvious: it is very difficult to prove a negative conclusively. . . .
> By looking at the number of murders committed while the

[1]Fortas, pp. 110-11.

death penalty was on the books and enforced, we can gain some indication of how many killers were obviously not deterred (because they committed murder).

However, there is absolutely no way that we can ever know, with any certainty, how many would-be murderers were in fact deterred from killing. By definition, they were deterred, they did not kill, and therefore we can never know what numbers to enter on that side of the statistical equation.

As the poet Hyman Barshay has vividly put it:

> The death penalty is a warning, just like a lighthouse throwing its beams out to sea. We hear about shipwrecks, but we do not hear about the ships the lighthouse guides safely on their way. We do not have proof of the number of ships it saves, but we do not tear the lighthouse down.[1]

Professor Charles Black of the Yale Law School, an ardent abolitionist, has described the statistical problem with finality:

> . . . after all possible inquiry, including the probing of all possible methods of inquiry, we do not know, and for systematic and easily visible reasons cannot know, what the truth about this "deterrent" effect may be. . . . A "scientific"—that is to say, a soundly based—conclusion is simply impossible, and no methodological path out of this tangle suggests itself.[2]

Furthermore, by way of answering the "non-deterrence" objection, we need to note that opponents of the death penalty focus attention on only one kind of criminal—that is, on those who commit murders in the heat of passion or irrationally (without thinking out the consequences which might follow from their criminal act). Karl Schuessler, for example, cites the case of convicted murderer Morris Wasser, who just prior to his execution reportedly said: "Well, this electrocution

---

[1]Carrington, pp. 82-83.
[2]Black, pp. 25-26. Black's basic objection is that "no adequately controlled experiment or observation is possible."

business is the bunk. It don't do no good, I tell you, and I know, because I never thought of the chair when I plugged that old guy. . . . I mean that you just don't think of the hot seat when you plug a guy. Somethin' inside you just makes you kill."[1] Such men, it is argued, are not deterred by the death penalty because they never think of the death penalty until the crime is over.

On the surface this seems to be a compelling argument against the deterrent influence of capital punishment. Yet is it true that the prospect of punishment has no deterrent effect on crimes of passion? Professor James Q. Wilson remarked:

> Such crimes of passion are not, as some claim, undeterrable. Even enraged persons are aware that their acts have some consequences, and it seems safe to assume that many more barroom or bedroom fights would end with a weapon being used if there were no penalty at all for the offense.[2]

At best, the argument that capital punishment does not deter crimes of passion focuses on only one kind of criminal. What of the criminal who premeditates his crime? Carrington observed:

> Capital punishment cannot and never will be able to deter *all* murderers. But this does not mean for a moment that it won't deter *any* murderers. When the criminal, particularly the murderer who *premeditates* his crime (the same murderer against whom most of the state capital murder statutes have been drawn) has an opportunity to weigh cost versus gain, cause and effect, he may well think twice if he knows that he will, in all likelihood, be put to death for his actions.

> This reasoning was sufficient to satisfy the United States Supreme Court in *Gregg vs. Georgia.* Justice Stewart held that:

[1] Karl F. Schuessler, "The Deterrent Influence of the Death Penalty," *Annals of the American Academy of Political and Social Science* 284 (November 1952), p. 63.
[2] Wilson, p. 151.

Although some of the studies suggest that the death penalty may not function as a significantly greater deterrent than lesser penalties, there is no convincing empirical evidence either supporting or refuting this view.

We may nevertheless assume safely that there are murderers, such as those who act in passion, for whom the threat of death has little or no deterrent effect. But for many others, the death penalty undoubtedly is a significant deterrent.[1]

For every Morris Wasser, there is an Orelius Steward, who, when he was arrested for attempted robbery in 1960, confessed: "The officer who arrested me was by himself, and if I had wanted, I could have blasted him. I thought about it at the time, but changed my mind when I thought of the gas chamber." And there are those like Louis Turck, who, though he had used a gun in robberies in other states, when arrested for a 1961 robbery in California, confessed that he only faked having a gun on that occasion because of the California death penalty law: "I knew that if I used a real gun and that if I shot someone in a robbery, I might get the death penalty and go to the gas chamber."[2]

There is one kind of criminal, of course, that the death penalty definitely deters. Surely it is clear to everyone who has common sense that capital punishment radically deters murderers from repeat offenses. How many victims of repeat offenders would still be alive if their murderers had been executed for previous murders? The answer is all of them! If a man is executed for his first murder, he will not live to murder again.

---

[1]Carrington, pp. 87-88.
[2]Ibid., p. 94.

Furthermore, in response to the so-called statistical argument for non-deterrence, we must recognize that if we follow such thinking to its logical conclusion, we would have to argue for the elimination of all penalties for violations of law. It could be argued, for example, that since the existing penalties do not restrain people from speeding on the highways, then we should eliminate or lessen those penalties. And this kind of reasoning could be applied to any law. And yet, as with the statistical methodology used by death penalty opponents, this thinking is based on a faulty methodology as well. We can only record statistics for those who are not deterred by the speeding laws; we have no statistics for the multitudes who are restrained out of fear of fines and arrest.

For the Christian, of course, the issue is not data or statistics or the opinions of sociologists and criminologists. For the Christian, no amount of negative data makes disobedience of God's Word an acceptable alternative. Furthermore, the Christian recognizes that the Bible teaches that the fear of punishment does deter. Romans 13:3-5 states:

> Rulers are not a terror to the good work, but to the evil. And wouldest thou have no fear of the power? do that which is good, and thou shalt have praise from the same: for he is a minister of God to thee for good. But if thou do that which is evil, be afraid; for he beareth not the sword in vain: for he is a minister of God, an avenger for wrath to him that doeth evil. Wherefore ye must needs be in subjection, not only because of the wrath, but also for conscience' sake.

While it is true that the Christian is to obey the law from a higher motive than fear of punishment (i.e., out of a sense of religious obligation to God—as the Apostle Paul says, "for conscience' sake"), nevertheless God has put the sword in the hand of the civil magistrate so that men will be deterred from doing evil.

Before leaving the deterrence issue, it is important to note that many opponents of the death penalty are not truly opposed to the death penalty as an appropriate deterrent to manslaying, at least not universally. The reason I say this is because, although they object to the execution of human murderers, they insist on the execution of animals which kill men. Let a pit bulldog or an alligator kill (or even attack) a child, and there is a public outcry for the death of such an obviously dangerous animal. And yet this demand for the execution of a dangerous animal is based on a reason which supposedly is invalid in the case of dangerous human man-slayers, i.e., as protection for the public. Such a bipolar perspective is unbiblical. As we saw earlier in our considera-tion of Genesis 9, the same penalty is to be levied against the manslayer, whether he is man or beast.

2. *It costs more to execute than to imprison for life.*

Opponents of the death penalty often argue that the death penalty is a poor use of public resources. Supposedly it is cheaper to imprison a murderer for life than to carry out the death penalty. The cost, of course, is not in the execution itself, but in the lengthy and expensive appeals process.

First, in response to this objection, we must recognize that in those states where the penalty for murder is life in prison, there is also a lengthy and expensive appeals process. Mur-derers sentenced to death are not the only murderers who appeal their convictions to the bitter end. Faced with a life of imprisonment, "lifers" also seek to exhaust their legal appeals. Therefore, if any system has the potential to be more costly, it is the "life sentence" system. Not only does the public bear the expense of the appeals process but also the expense of a lifetime of maintenance for the "lifer" in a high security prison.

Second, even if the death penalty is more expensive, are we as a society prepared to start down the slippery slope of equating justice with money? What are we prepared to pay to do God's clearly revealed will? Surely, when compared with the mind of God revealed in the Bible, the so-called "cost" argument is irrelevant for the Christian.

3. A mandatory death penalty makes convictions harder to win.

Opponents of the death penalty often argue that the death penalty (especially where it is mandatory by statute) makes prosecution more difficult. Supposedly jurors are reluctant to convict, knowing that a vote for conviction may lead to execution. This, of course, would be true if jurors weren't carefully screened. In many jurisdictions, however, a screening process is used to excuse from capital cases jurors who oppose the death penalty. This procedure greatly reduces the problem of jurors who are unwilling to convict in capital cases. In any case, as with the preceding pragmatic objections, for the Christian this objection can have no weight when stacked against God's will revealed in his Word.

Concluding Observations

IN THE PRECEDING pages we have surveyed the biblical materials and considered the primary objections raised against the biblical teaching on the death penalty. As we come now to the end of our study, I want to conclude with several observations.

1. *Beware of the evil fruit of not punishing evil-doers.*

As the people of God we must warn our nation about the terrible results of not punishing evil-doers (especially of not executing murderers). Unprincipled and unbiblical leniency to criminals produces contempt for the laws of God and for the laws of society and the end result is more evil-doing. Crime is on the rise because (among other reasons) criminals do not fear a judicial system without real teeth. As wise King Solomon observed, "Because sentence against an evil work is not executed speedily, therefore the heart of the sons of men is fully set in them to do evil" (Ecclesiastes 8:11). Criminals will be deterred only when punishment is swift, sure, and commensurate with the evil done.

Our nation needs to be warned that it is subject to (indeed already under) the wrath of God because of injustice in the land. As in the case of the blood of Abel, all across our country the voice of innocent blood cries to God for vengeance. We need to say to our neighbors and to our leaders that when men take away justice, there is One higher than the high who regards it (Ecclesiastes 5:8). God sees and takes account of how men live; and he judges nations according to whether they are just or unjust. And although America is not Old Covenant Israel, we need to take to heart the principle which God revealed in Numbers 35:33, "Ye shall not pollute the land wherein ye are: for blood, it polluteth the land; and no expiation can be made for the land for the blood that is shed therein, but by the blood of him that shed it." America is polluted by the blood of multitudes whose murders have never been avenged, including the blood of millions who have been slaughtered in their mothers' wombs. If we do not cleanse the land by justice, God will cleanse it by judgment!

2. *What can Christians do?*

What can Christians do to influence the present situation in our land? Certainly, as private citizens we can exercise our legal rights and seek to influence our civil rulers and fellow citizens. We can inform them of the true teaching of the Word of God—no small service in a generation where the society at large is woefully ignorant of the biblical teaching on capital punishment. The Christian is also at liberty to lobby legislators and other public officials to change statutes and practices which are at variance with biblical principles. The most effective thing, however, that Christians can do is pray! The Apostle Paul writes, "I exhort therefore, first of all, that supplications, prayers, intercessions, thanksgivings, be made for all men; for kings and all that are in high place; that we may lead a tranquil and quiet life in all godliness and gravity" (1 Timothy 2:1-2).

Certainly, the consistent application of a righteous penal code (and the deterrent effect which this would have on evildoers) is no small part of what is needed if we are to live tranquil and quiet lives. Our civil rulers need conviction and wisdom and courage to frame and to implement such a code; and the only One who can give them these virtues is God himself. Therefore, as Christians, desirous of living tranquil and quiet lives, we must pray "for kings and all that are in high place" that God will work mightily in their hearts and minds and consciences. And we can pray in confidence that our God is able to answer our prayers, for, as Proverbs 21:1 affirms, "The king's heart is in the hand of Jehovah as the watercourses: he turneth it whithersoever he will."

3. *Executions should be times of public soberness.*

Where capital punishment is carried out in our society, although we should be thankful to see God's will implemented, these occasions ought to be times of soberness and grief, especially among the people of God. These should not be seasons for the expression of a carnal spirit of self-righteousness or vengeance. This writer will not soon forget the pictures of cheering spectators outside the penitentiary where Theodore Bundy was executed. Such ungodly spectacles ought never to be seen in the land. Rather, as imagebearers of God, we should be like our Creator who takes no pleasure in the death of the wicked (cf., Ezekiel 18:23,32; 33:11). When a criminal is executed, it ought to be an occasion of mourning, as we grieve that a wicked man must be cut off in his sin.

4. *Christian, search the Scriptures.*

In conclusion, I trust that the reader will bear with a final exhortation. I have tried comprehensively and fairly to present the biblical data on the subject of capital punishment and to consider carefully the objections which have been raised against the biblical doctrine. All that I can reasonably ask of you, the reader, is that you will carefully and prayerfully consider what I have written. Ultimately, however, you must wrestle with your own conscience before the Word of God and before the God of the Word. My final exhortation to all who read this book is, *Search the Scriptures*, whether the things which I have written are so (cf., Acts 17:11). I believe that an honest and unbiased study of the Bible will demonstrate that indeed capital punishment is God's will and not man's folly.

The Death Penalty: God's Will or Man's Folly

Cover designed by Benjamin W. Geist
Composed by Simpson Graphics
Printed by Bookcrafters

SIMPSON
PUBLISHING COMPANY
The righteous are bold as a lion - *Proverbs 28:1*